Bible Study for the 21st Century

Bible Study for the 21st Century

Lucas Grollenberg OP

translated from the third revised edition
by
John E. Steely
Southeastern Baptist Theological Seminary

TRANSLATOR'S PREFACE

Unavoidable delays in the publication of this translation have served to confirm the worth of the book. It is as timely now as when it first appeared in Dutch in 1971. My own enthusiasm for its publication in translation is based on the intrinsic value of this stimulating treatment of a perennial question. In addition, I am glad to be able to share in a task that involves Catholic and Protestant, European and North American Christians alike, thus fulfilling the author's and the publishers' original ecumenical intention.

Many unnamed persons have had a part in making this publication possible. I should like to express my gratitude to the staff of the Library of Southeastern Baptist Theological Seminary, for their patience, resourcefulness, and generosity in responding to my frequent requests for assistance. My greatest debt of gratitude is owed, as always, to my family, for their encouragement and for help on many of the specific tasks involved in bringing this work to completion.

John E. Steely

Wake Forest, North Carolina
September 1975

FOREWORD

What is the significance of modern biblical exposition for the Oekoumene?* This little book attempts to sketch an answer to this question. It appeared to me to be useful to show how the traditional idea of inspiration arose and functioned throughout the centuries (chapter I). This can help to explain why so much resistance came from the churches to historical criticism, of which I sketch the first characteristics by way of a couple of examples (chapter II). The only way out of the impasse that developed thereby appears to me to lead to the Oekoumene (chapter III).

This plan has led me into several areas other than that in which I feel at home. One should therefore regard this little book as a tentative effort, a contribution to discussion. In order to make the reading easier, in the text I have avoided anything that could arouse the impression of technical scholarship. The reader who wishes to know the precise source of citations can find that information at the end of the book in the notes.

I am glad to express my thanks here to Ton van der Worp for his stimulating companionship, my confrater Jan Groot for his help, and Harry Huisintveld for his tireless work with the typing.

Lucas Grollenberg

---

*This term, identifying the series in which this book first appeared in Dutch, transliterates the Greek word meaning "the inhabited earth." In this respect it connotes universality. From the same Greek word comes the adjective "ecumenical." As used here and elsewhere in this book, "oecumene" means the totality of Christendom, united not divided.

Table of Contents

1

Inspired Books
And Their Interpretation

"The first thing God created was a pen. The pen asked, 'What am I to do?' He answered, 'Write!' The pen said, 'What must I write?' Then God said, 'Write the story of what is to befall all things, down to the last day.'"

In this story God is called "Allah." It refers to the holy book of the Moslems, the Koran. Actually this book came into being by stages. Shortly after the year 610, Mohammed began to call his fellow-citizens in Mecca to repentance. The end of the world was near. As evidence of this the prophet appealed to appearances of the angel Gabriel. Some of the "revelations" uttered by Mohammed were already written down during his lifetime. Just after his death, in 632, disciples brought together the literary and orally preserved utterances in a book, "the book" of the Moslems. This quickly came to be regarded as a great miracle of Allah, and as a proof of Mohammed's divine mission.

People expressed this reverence for the Koran by giving "the book" a directly divine origin, as in the story above. The Koran must have existed before all other things. Islamic thinkers even came to the position that the Koran is eternal and uncreated, for this book *is* the utterance of God himself. Everything of God is eternal; therefore even his speaking, and thus also the Koran....

A similar train of thought had been developed earlier by

Judaism. Those who are familiar with other religions and cultures tell us of similar phenomena. Whenever a community begins to venerate a particular writing as holy, two things appear always to happen. The people who brought the text into being are quickly forgotten, or at least are no longer seen. It is as though they are outshone by the divine light that shines forth from the written words, flooding the believers. These are, after all, taken as words from the deity itself. Thus "the Book" is actually brought into being in the divine world. If the human writer still is spoken of, he is identified as an "inspired" person: what he wrote down was "breathed into" him from above (*inspiration* means "in-breathing") or was dictated to him by a heavenly voice, or he copied it from a heavenly text which was shown to him in visions.

This is one consequence of the sanctification of a text. Another consists in the fact that from then on, no one is authorized to change anything in the text. The "letter" is forever fixed. But like everything else in this world, the community in which "the holy Book" functions is subject to change. Social developments take place, new insights break through, customs give way to others. In order to be able to gain acceptance by the believing community, all this that is new must be clothed with divine authority. It must all stand in the holy book. Hence that second phenomenon: there arises an exposition of the holy scripture, an exposition that changes with the times, and that in each new period defines the "spirit" in which the "letter" must be understood.

In this chapter we confine ourselves to the fortunes of the books that have been declared holy in the Jewish and Christian communities. For our subject is to be the Bible. Many a reader will encounter expressions and "explanations" which will surprise him, and which he perhaps will spontaneously label foolish or ridiculous. That would be a pity, for the believing people of antiquity who will be discussed in the following pages were not dumber or less rational than ourselves. They only had different ways of giving expression to ideas and feelings concerning that which makes meaning and sense out of human life.

1. Judaism and its holy book

In the Israel of David and Solomon much writing was done, but it did not yet possess a generally recognized holy book. The art of writing there had the same functions as in any other developed society. David in his brand-new kingdom naturally decided to organize a census, with a view to taxation and military service. In that connection records had to be made of everyone. For this purpose David had recourse to trained officials from abroad, primarily from Egypt. He also sent Judeans thither to get training in specific functions. Thus the new capital city Jerusalem very quickly gained a considerable number of educated men, among them professional scribes. Among the clerks and secretaries were some who cherished literature and even themselves produced, in Hebrew, "belles-lettres." It was probably someone from their circles who wrote the pretty "novella" of Joseph in Egypt. The reign of David's son and successor Solomon qualifies as the first flowering of Hebrew literature. A masterwork from this time is the story that tells under what circumstances David got his son Solomon and through what political entanglements the latter came to his father's throne. This splendid piece of literature was preserved for us because it came to rest in the Bible (II Sam. 9-20, with the continuation and conclusion in I Kings 1-2). But when it was written, it was ordinary literature. The same is true of the more expressly religious work of the so-called Jahwist; we shall say more about this in the third chapter.

It is true that in the many sacred places of Israel, larger and smaller temples, there were writings with a religious character preserved and used, such as texts with sacred narratives, descriptions of rites, and liturgical songs. But they did not function as holy books in the sense that they determine the life of the entire community.

All this continued to be true when after Solomon's death (abut 930 B. C.) the kingdom divided into two parts, the large northern state of Israel and the smaller Judah with its capital Jerusalem. In these societies all sorts of things were written, on all kinds of material. Receipts and brief communications sometimes on broken bits of pottery; letters, contracts, reports, annals, and belles-lettres on sheets of papyrus which were imported from Egypt. Where enough money was available, people wrote on treated animal skins, parchments. Inks of various kinds were available. These writing materials were used also by the priests who were connected with the shrines, not only national temples like that of Jerusalem in the south and that of Dan in the northern kingdom, but in other places as well. Certainly the prophets Elijah and Elisha were acquainted with traditions from Israel's past, some of which also possibly had been put down in writing. Among these were stories, about the tribal patriarchs and about the exodus from Egypt, as well as collections of legal rules and prescriptions.

In 721 B. C. the state of Israel was swept off the map with a harsh hand by the invading Assyrians. They scattered members of the leading classes over their immense world empire, and replaced these with colonists from the homeland of Assyria. These naturally brought with them their gods and rites and priests. It is almost certain that in these years a number of faithful worshippers of Jahweh, who remained devoted to Israel's oldest traditions, sought refuge in Judah and took with them what had been handed down to them, also in written form. We do not know how they implanted and inculcated these there. But a century later King Josiah profited from their zeal. When the Assyrian power went into grave decline, this king (about 640-609) began to think of a major restoration of the nation. This had to include a thoroughgoing renewal of religion. The temple in Jerusalem, in preceding years defaced and desecrated by all sorts of intrusions from other religions, was thoroughly purified and

restored. In this process someone found a lawbook that went
back to ancient traditions, evidently the work of men who at
one time had come from the old heart of the country, the
region around Shechem. On the basis of this text, approximately like what now forms the kernel of the biblical book of
Deuteronomy (chapters 12-26), King Josiah carried through
his reforms. The people of Judah had to rediscover their true
unity, their "identity," by unitedly worshipping their one
God at only one place, the temple in Jerusalem. Thus Josiah
breathed new life into the age-old concept of the "covenant."
In this undertaking he was assisted by all sorts of "sages,"
men who knew something of the past, had access to archives,
and could write. They assembled all sorts of documentation
into a kind of historical work, something like a national epic.
They framed the newly discovered lawbook, which bore
Moses' name, with addresses and "sermons" of Moses. He
promised prosperity whenever the people would live in faithful observance of his laws and ordinances, and he threatened
them with frightful disasters and total destruction whenever
they should forget their covenant with Jahweh. They had this
introduction followed by the "history" which we know from
our biblical books of Joshua, Judges, Samuel, and Kings.
Therein they had so arranged, touched up, and supplemented
the available material that it let the reader see clearly how the
principles of "Moses," blessing and curse, had been at work
throughout all this history.

This great work still could not then become "holy
scripture." The necessary pre-conditions for this development still were lacking. Religion was one of the many
expressions of life of a community which had a king, an
army, diplomats, agriculture, industry, and commerce. The
Babylonians were quickly to put an end to this variegated
life. They had taken over the waning empire of the Assyrians
and now in turn they began to develop their power in the
direction of enticing Egypt. In 597 they captured Jerusalem
and deported a part of the leading classes to Babylon. It

seemed best to them to let Judah continue to exist as a tributary kingdom. But Judah turned out not to be a reliable vassal. In 587 the Babylonians totally destroyed it, and therewith created the pre-conditions in which Judaism could arise.

The priest-prophet Ezekiel is regarded as the founder of Judaism. He taught the disillusioned exiles from Judah how they could practice their old faith in this new set of circumstances. An end now had come to the diverse and varied life of the nation with which it earlier had formed a whole. But Jahweh was not bound to land and temple. Ezekiel had seen the divine glory leave the temple and had beheld it in the midst of the Babylonian land. One could also meet Jahweh there. And people could unite in usages and rites which were not coupled to a locally determined sacrificial worship. Thus there in Babylon the Sabbath acquired a new community-forming significance. A man who took employment with a Babylonian employer would be conspicuous because of his having been circumcised, for that custom was unknown in this area. Thus it became for the Jews a symbol of their belonging together, a token of the covenant. In the same way a bond was formed among people who for the sake of Jahweh abstained from certain foods which were commonly eaten in Babylonia.

Although we do not know much about the life of the exiles, it is certain that during their weekly gatherings they occupied themselves with what they had brought with them out of the ruins of the city and the temple: recollections of Israel's past, formulations in which the faith was earlier uttered and sometimes even written down. They reflected on the threatening utterances of various prophets, which had come to pass. Thus their word had been an authentic word of God. New inspired persons, such as Ezekiel and the poet of Isaiah 40-55, added their messages from God to these. Priests, now freed from their numerous duties in the temple, pored over ancient ritual texts and edited them, with an eye to a hoped-for new liturgy in Jerusalem, in the new spirit of remorse and repentance. In this way there developed all sorts of texts which later would become "holy scripture."

With all this, many Judeans became more and more firmly rooted in the Babylonian soil. When Cyrus conquered Babylon and gave permission to all those who had been deported to return to their homeland together with their gods, only relatively few Judeans heeded the appeal of their leaders. Thus it was that the community which then developed in and around Jerusalem led a somewhat poor and skimpy existence. As a modern historian of Israel expresses it: "The new Israel desperately wanted something to draw it together and give it distinctive identity." The man who fulfilled this need was Ezra. On the authority of the Persian rulers this scribe brought to Jerusalem a lawbook which had been prepared in Babylonia. Unfortunately the exact date is unknown. Some would place it in 398 B. C., and others prefer the date of 458 or 428. What is certain is that the solemn acceptance of the lawbook by the people, as it is described in Nehemiah 8, became a turning-point, and this is sometimes regarded as the *dies natalis*, the birthdate, of Judaism, of which Ezra then is often called the father. This event led to a new definition of the concept "Israel." Once again to quote the above-mentioned historian:

"Israel would no longer be a national entity, nor one coterminous with the descendants of the Israelite tribes or the inhabitants of the old national territory, nor even a community of those who in some way acknowledged Jahweh as God and offered him worship. From now on, Israel would be viewed (as in the theology of the Chronicler) as that remnant of Judah which had rallied around the law. He would be a member of Israel (i.e., a Jew) who assumed the burden of the law.

But this redefinition of Israel meant inevitably the emergence of a religion in which law was central. This betokened, let it be repeated, no break with Israel's ancient faith, all the major features of which continued in force, but a radical regrouping of that faith about the law. The law no longer merely regulated the affairs of an already constituted community; it had created the community!"

It is not certain whether the lawbook that Ezra brought already had the form of the "five books of Moses" or the "Pentateuch" in our Bibles. According to some investigators this form came into being only in the course of the fourth century. Be that as it may, in the succeeding centuries we see the veneration for that "holy book" expressed in ever increasing measure, while at the same time methods were being developed to interpret that word of God with regard to the problems and according to the insights of the respective times.

2. Divine words written down by Moses

Shortly after the year 200 B. C., a wise teacher in Jerusalem, Jesus, son of Sirach, wrote about the divine wisdom which was the actual source from which he drew all that he put into words that was worthwhile. In imitation of the Book of Proverbs (chapter 8), he portrays wisdom as a female being which came forth from God before all things and was with God when he made the universe, the heavens and the earth and all the nations that dwell on the earth. "Then I began to seek among all these people a dwelling-place," the woman Wisdom relates, "and finally the Creator himself directed me: 'You must go to dwell in Israel....' So I established myself in Jerusalem....I flourished there as a fragrant plant...."

"I am the mother of fair love,
Of the fear of God, of knowledge, and of holy hope;
In me is all the grace of life and truth,
In me all hope of life and virtue.
Come to me, you who desire me,
And be satisfied with my fruits....
Anyone who listens to me will never be ashamed,
And he who labors for me will not sin."

In a somewhat jarring fashion for our feeling, immediately
after these lofty poetic verses there follows the comment of
the writer:

"All this is the book of the covenant of the Most High,
The Law which Moses gave as an inheritance for Jacob's
communities."

For Jesus Sirach, the scribe, the law of Moses is nothing
less than the eternal wisdom now become a book.

Written perhaps somewhat later is a passage from the brief
writing which carries the name of Baruch and which is
usually placed in the Greek (and Catholic) Bibles after
Jeremiah and Lamentations. The author treats the same
subject as does chapter 28 of the Book of Job: wherever man
may seek, the way to wisdom is hidden from him:

"No one knows her ways,
No one is familiar with her paths.
Only he who knows all things knows her;
He found her out with his understanding.
He who founded the earth for evermore,
And filled it with the beasts;
He who sends forth the light, and it goes,
Who calls it back, and it obeys him with fear.
The stars flicker on their guardposts,
And shine with joy.
When he calls them, they say, 'Here we are!'
They shine with joy before him who made them.
This is our God;
No one else is like unto him!
He has searched out all the ways of wisdom,
And has revealed her to Jacob his servant,
And to Israel his people.
Then she appeared upon earth
And had commerce with men.
She is the book of God's commandments,
The law that endures forever!"

The poem ends with an exhortation to Israel to live in the
light of the law, to hold it fast, and not to give the divine

glory to others. "Israel, how happy we are, because what is pleasing to God is made known to us."

In this way the idea could arise that the law also existed with God before all things. This was expressed in all sorts of ways. "When God said, 'Let *us* make man,' he was speaking to the Torah." It was also said that God has created the world "for the sake of the Torah," and the Torah was even regarded by some as the instrument of creation: the world is created by her. Hence statements like the following: "Anyone who affirms that the Torah did not come from heaven shall have no part in the world to come," and "Anyone who says that Moses wrote even a single line on his own authority is a liar and holds God's word in contempt."

Sometimes "Torah" can have approximately the meaning of "revelation." But in many of the expressions of this sort people clearly have in view the book, the Pentateuch. The last lines of the Pentateuch describe the death of Moses. Even these sentences were "given" to him, whether they were dictated to him, or whether he copied them from the heavenly texts which were shown to him.

The idea of a text existing in heaven on heavenly "tablets" is found in a writing that was very popular in Jesus' day, certainly in some circles. The best known title is "The Book of (the) Jubilees." This is a kind of biblical history. In his own way the writer relates the contents of the book of Genesis and the beginning of Exodus, as far as Sinai. In his own way: first of all, he is strongly interested in calculating times. He divides the time since creation into periods of 49 years, seven times seven, "jubilees." On the basis of this calculation he gives precise dates of all events. After Adam had lived in Paradise seven years, "in the second month, on the seventeenth day, the serpent came and approached Eve...." We shall return later to this interest in dates. What concerns us here is what the writer and his milieu thought about the law. Written down on heavenly tablets already before creation, it has been in force since the beginning and will always remain in force. Even the highest angels observe the Sabbath with joy, obedient to the most fundamental commandment of the Torah. Once he has left Paradise, Adam presents a fragrant offering of incense every morning, prepared in accordance with Exodus 30:34. Abraham celebrated the Feast of Tabernacles according to the way in which the prescriptions of the law were practiced in the milieu of the writer.

What he does not tell from the book of Genesis are the less attractive deeds of Israel's patriarchs, such as the lies of Abraham and Isaac with reference to their wives, the deceit practiced by Jacob upon Laban, and Jacob's fear of his brother Esau. He even pronounces some of these deeds good. Thus according to him, Simeon and Levi did a praiseworthy work when they massacred the populace of Shechem; indeed, it was because of this action that Levi and his tribe were chosen for the priesthood. The writer also will know nothing of a reconciliation between Jacob and his brother Esau. On the contrary, he has Esau killed by Jacob's own hand. This is in line with what he earlier has had their old blind father Isaac say to Esau: "If you throw off his (Jacob's) yoke, you will be committing a sin unto death and your posterity will be blotted out."

This seems strange to us. On the one hand the Torah is a book that is written in heaven, and on the other hand the writer alters the details of the Genesis-stories whenever it suits him. At the root of this contradiction lies an ardent belief in the unique role of "Israel." On the basis of this belief, the Law upon which the Jewish community is based becomes an absolute, divine entity, and at the same time everything that lies outside this community is rejected (Esau = Edom = embodiment of what is non-Jewish, heathendom; Shechem = the Samaritans = even worse than the heathen). To put it in another way: the author is writing from within and on behalf of a community which can maintain her identity only by experiencing a unique bond with the only true God and the almost fanatical rejection of what the "world," in fact the brilliant and worldwide culture of Hellenism, has to offer by way of "wisdom" and universal humanity.

3. An "inspired" translation

People naturally thought of the heavenly tables which Moses copied as having been written in the Hebrew language. God and his angels converse in this language. So did Adam and Eve. But how was the divine law now to be read among Jews who already for generations had been living in a Greek-speaking environment and no longer understood the language of the Torah?

This problem first presented itself in Egypt. Already before the disaster of 587 people from Judah had emigrated thither. After this event still others came. We know that some went into military service, for even before the invasion of Egypt by the Persian prince Cambyses (525 B. C.) there existed a military colony on the island Elephantine in the Nile near the present Aswan, with a garrison of Jewish mercenaries. There they had built a temple for their God "Jaho." Excavations there have brought to light letters from which it appears that this temple was destroyed in 410 at the instigation of Egyptian priests, and was restored a few years later. These Jews spoke and wrote Aramaic.

While beginning in the sixth century B. C. there were also many colonists from Greece who had come to dwell in the Nile delta, after the conquest by Alexander the Great Greek became more and more the common language, certainly in the rapidly growing capital city which the conquerer had founded, Alexandria. His successors, the brilliant Ptolemies, did everything possible to make this city the greatest center of culture and technology in the entire known world. In the time of its greatest flourishing it must have had almost a million inhabitants. Among these were tens of thousands of Jews. These had their own quarter of the city, but many of them lived elsewhere in the city, where their offices and synagogues also were scattered. As a religious group they had their own governing body, a kind of council of elders, with an *ethnarch*, a ruler of the people, at its head. They regarded the Jews who still lived in Palestine as their brethren, and for Jerusalem with its temple they cherished a profound veneration.

There were also scholars and scribes among the Jews of Alexandria. The first Ptolemy had already begun to draw scientists and scholars from the whole world, not only literary figures but also astronomers, geographers, physicians, and historians. He provided them royally with all that they needed for their scientific investigations. The first Ptolemy also laid the foundation for the library of Alexandria that became so famous, which about 235 B. C. possessed 490,000 volumes in scrolls. One could find there the whole of Greek literature, but also translations of ancient works from Egypt and Babylonia. Even writings from faraway India found their way into this collection, the greatest the world knew before the invention of the printing art.

In that milieu it was not difficult to fulfill the wishes of the synagogue worshippers and to replace the more or less spontaneous translations of passages from the Torah with a generally recognized Greek text of the entire divine work of Moses. This was a genuine translation, in the sense that the meaning of the Hebrew was reproduced in the conceptual world of the translators. To take one example that recently came up in a discussion of abortion: an ancient law in the book of Exodus concerns the case where a pregnant woman becomes involved in a fight between men and suffers a blow which causes a miscarriage. The Hebrew text, which is not entirely clear, seems to say that if the blow is not fatal for the woman, the one who struck her can make amends with a fine, but if she dies, then the rule of "a life for a life" is in force. The translator has more interest in the child. According to the science of his time, one can regard a male fetus as "formed" after forty days, and a female fetus after ninety days. He has Moses decree: "if her child comes forth not yet formed, he (the one who struck the blow) shall pay a fine . . . ; but if it was formed, then he shall pay his life for the life . . . ."

Thus it was a genuine "translation." But a great many Jews still had difficulty with this. Should the wisdom which God had granted to Israel alone now simply be made accessible to outsiders, heathen? *Can* it in fact be reproduced in a language which actually had nothing to do with the revelation? In order to meet these difficulties, an Alexandrian Jew in the course of the second century B. C. wrote the little book which is preserved for us under the title of "The epistle of Aristeas."

The writer tells a certain Philocrates how he was sent by King Ptolemy (305-282) to the high priest in Jerusalem to confer about a translation of the Law. He, Aristeas, was himself present when the first librarian of Alexandria informed the king that there was still a Jewish book in Jerusalem, written in Hebrew letters on parchment, which should be made accessible also in Greek. After a digression about Jewish captives who through his intervention were set free, Aristeas tells how he, with another high official named Andreas, came to the high priest Eleazar. They presented to him the king's request that he send a number of translators, who should be both virtuous and knowledgeable, with a copy of the Hebrew law to Egypt. The high priest accepts the costly gifts which the king has sent along, and chooses from each of the twelve tribes six biblical scholars who are very well acquainted with the Greek language and culture. After Aristeas has a long talk with them about the meaning of the prohibition of eating certain animals, he departs with the chosen translators for Alexandria. Contrary to the standard protocol — which prescribed a waiting period of several days — these guests were received immediately by the great king, who bowed seven times before the divine text, had his guests installed in comfortable quarters, and then gave a banquet in their honor which lasted for seven days. Each day the ruler queried ten of his guests about the work and obligations of a king, who according to the Hellenistic ideals ought to be a thoroughly virtuous and wise man. The chosen translators appear to be marvelously well informed on such matters. "Aristeas" repeats all their wise answers. After three days the seventy-two men set to work on a quiet island, and "it came to pass that the work of translation was completed in exactly seventy-two days, as though an exact schedule had been set for it." The text was read aloud in the presence of the Jewish community and was enthusiastically approved. This was henceforward to be the Torah text, not a single letter of which might be altered. The writer tells how people who had used passages from the Torah in their own translations were punished for this by God, with mental disorders and blindness. Finally the translators, under royal escort and laden with gifts for the high priest, return to Jerusalem.

Thus the synagogue's worshippers can be reassured. The generally used Greek text is the best conceivable translation, done under the patronage of the great Ptolemy, made by scholars from all the tribes of Israel, chosen by the high priest himself; and they worked in the most ideal atmosphere, both quiet and scholarly, of Alexandria, where they miraculously completed their work in seventy-two days.

The story accomplished its purpose beautifully. This is evident from the further developments which it underwent. The great Jewish philosopher Philo (about 13 B. C.-A. D. 45) tells it in his own way, with still more marvelous things. Thus the high priest of Jerusalem, now also "king" of the Jews, recognizes in the request of Ptolemy, the greatest ruler of all times, a clear sign from God. The seventy-two translators begin their work on the Island Pharos with intense prayer and then begin to write under divine inspiration. For each of them separately makes a translation of the entire Law, and upon comparison when they have finished, it turns out that their seventy-two texts are in exact agreement, to the very last letter. Considering the large vocabulary in Greek, says Philo, it is clear that these men did not work merely as scholars, but that the words "were breathed into them as by an invisible person." Actually they were not translators, but "hierophants (priests who disclose divine things) and prophets." Philo also relates that at that time a festival was instituted, celebrated yearly on the island, commemorating the miracle of the translation that had occurred there. We could also give a selection from early Christian writers who took over the story with all sorts of variations and ornamentations. This appropriation was understandable, because the Greek translation of the Jewish writings was fundamental for them; with the help of this text they "proved" the divine truth of their new faith. But for this very reason the "Septuagint" (the translation of the *seventy*) quickly fell into disuse among the Jews. They had much more literal translations of the Hebrew Torah made, in order to strengthen their stand in their disputes with the Christians. They finally gave up the Greek. Thus it came about that the yearly Septuagint-festival among the Jews was changed into a day of fasting and repentance, a recollection of the disastrous moment in which the divine Torah was delivered to unbelieving people.

4. Methods of interpretation

After the Torah, quickly divided into five books, the Jews accepted two other collections of writings as sacred, sharing in the holy character of the Torah. These were "the prophets" and "the writings." They too came from God, and the writers were like Moses; all of them were "inspired." The successor whom Moses had appointed at God's command, Joshua, stood close enough to this original source of all inspiration to qualify as the writer of the book of which he himself was the hero and which came to bear his name, the book of Joshua. The great prophet Samuel had written the book of Judges and the work that followed it and that was named for him.

Jeremiah was regarded as the writer of Kings. The so-called "later" prophets were each one written by the spokesmen of God for whom they were named, the books of Isaiah, Jeremiah, Ezekiel, and the twelve (minor prophets). The various "writings" also came from inspired men. The wisdom which Solomon put down in Proverbs and Ecclesiastes was breathed into him, at his request, by God himself. David, who was changed into a different person by the spirit of God, was the inspired author of the Psalms. Actually this book contained all sorts of liturgical poems which had arisen in the course of centuries, combined by groups, finally to be fixed about 250 B. C., in the large complete book that divided the 150 Psalms into five "books," just like the Torah. But the historical origin was quickly forgotten in order to make a place for the conviction that David was the inspired writer of the Psalms. When the 150 poems were fixed into a single book, David's name was already set above 73 of them. In the superscription of some, even the circumstances of composition were related, for example "when the prophet Nathan came to him after he had gone in to Bathsheba" (Psalm 51), and "when he sat in the cave, when he was fleeing from Saul" (Psalm 57). In the Greek translation of the book this conviction was expressed even more strongly; there David's name stands above 84 Psalms, while there is added a one-hundred-fifty-first under the title, "Written by David himself when he fought with Goliath."

Yet in none of these cases is the "inspiration" so perfect as in the case of the Torah. First of all, for that divine book the principle holds true that *everything is included in it*. If this text existed before all things, if the Torah was the instrument of creation, and if its words are to remain even when heaven and earth shall have passed away, then this principle is not unreasonable. Then everything that can be known about the world and about what happens in the world must be contained in this text. Then it must contain all true wisdom of all times. Then not even a letter or mark of it can be without profound meaning. Then a person may rightly devote an entire lifetime to the development and application of methods in order to wrest from the divine text an insight into the mysteries of the world and of life.

This view is still alive in our own times. This is evident in a book which appeared in 1963 in The Hague, The Netherlands, under the title, *De Bijbel als schepping* ("The Bible as Creation"). In this title the word "Bible" does not mean what it always is understood in the Christian world to mean, the whole of the Old and New Testaments, but only the Torah. The author, F. Weinreb, believes in the divine origin of that book in the way described above. The order of creation must be discoverable in this text; all the secrets of the cosmos and of human life are contained in it. Of course the real, most profound meanings do not emerge in an ordinary reading. For this a key is necessary. Weinreb possesses this key, made available to him through Jewish groups who have handed it down from generation to generation.

The key is this: each letter of the Hebrew alphabet has also a numerical value: *aleph* stands for 1, *beth* for 2, *gimel* for 3, and so on. Now when one calculates the value of certain words in a story from the Torah, one discovers marvelous connections. The Hebrew word that refers to the "mist" which according to the creation narrative (Gen. 2:5) arises from the earth consists of two letters with the values 1 and 4. Then the four rivers of Paradise also flow forth from it. The word for "man," with three letters, 1, 4, and 40, has the same structure. The human situation is also marked by this same number four; for the letters of "the tree of the knowledge of good and evil," totalling 932, have exactly four times the value of "the tree of life," 233.

What appears to the reader an ordinary historical sketch conceals, according to this interpretation, much deeper meanings. Thus Abraham pitched his tent between Bethel and Ai (Gen. 12:8). If one subtracts Ai from Bethel, the result is 358, and that is also the cipher-value of the word "Messiah." Moreover, when the tent stood halfway between these two places, the distance was half of 358, or 179, and that is the value of "garden of Eden," Paradise. Weinreb summarizes thus: "In fact, after this life of making ridiculous and smashing human gods, Abraham comes to the place which is the garden of Eden, on the way which is the way of the Messiah."

Weinreb says that in his book (of almost 600 pages) he gives only a small sampling of all the mysteries which can be discovered in the Torah in this fashion. The presupposition is a text that was fixed by God in the very beginning. In the light of this point of departure, then, Weinreb can write: "Therefore not a jot or a tittle in the Bible may be changed. If that were done, the whole structure would collapse. And then there would in fact remain nothing more than a 'story.'"

Even before the beginning of the Christian era, Jewish scribes were speculating with the help of the numerical value of Hebrew letters and words, and there are traces of such to be found in the sacred books themselves. As far as our subject is concerned, it is Weinreb's presupposition that is of primary importance: the Torah is of divine origin, and therefore it contains all knowledge. Not only so, but deeper things also must lie concealed in texts which at first glance are not profound, appear pedestrian, contain contradictions, or in some other way are unworthy of God. It is obvious that here the standards of the reader, the interpreter, and their milieu hold sway. What they expect of a book written by God must be discoverable therein.

Take an example from the "epistle of Aristeas" which was mentioned earlier. Aristeas tells that he had a conversation in Jerusalem about certain prescriptions of the divine law. He repeats this in detail as a part of his defense of the Jewish manner of life against objections which are raised from the perspective of "a sound reason," as this was understood in Alexandria at that time. "Our wise lawgiver, said the high priest, equipped by God with the knowledge of all things, has surrounded us with unbroken hedges and with walls of iron, that we should in no way mingle with the other nations, remaining pure in body and soul, free of unworthy opinions, worshiping the only and almighty God and no creature at all." Then he explains why the network of prescriptions with which God has surrounded the Jews, his true servants, also contains rules about the eating of animals. Moses (in the laws of Leviticus 11 and Deuteronomy 14) actually was not concerned about weasels and rats. His concern was simply with morality. Notice: the fowls which may be eaten are domesticated and clean, because they feed on seed and green things; fowls such as doves, partridges, and geese. Forbidden are wild and savage fowls, which contrary to all right feed on domestic animals, even stealing sheep and goats, and sometimes attack men, both living and dead. In forbidding these, Moses wanted to impress upon us "that we must consider righteousness, never do violence to another man, and steal nothing...." The characteristic marks which he gives, such as "with cloven hoof" and "chewing the cud," are also meant in the moral sense; he is concerned with the avoidance of bad company and the constant reflection, "rumination," upon the great deeds which God has wrought for his people.

With this we approach the world of the great Jewish philosopher Philo. We have already seen that for him the Greek translation of the Torah was not merely authoritative, but word-for-word, and even letter-by-letter "inspired." This conviction was connected with his manner of philosophizing. He was intensely involved in an intellectual world in which the formerly divergent tendencies of thought of the Greeks, those of Plato, the Stoa, and the Pythagoreans, met and influenced each other. What Philo as a Jewish thinker dug up out of this mixture by way of true insights he wanted to find confirmed in his holy scripture. This was not pioneering work, for in the Greek world also there were ancient texts which were regarded as inspired. Had not Homer often invoked the muse? Other poets also were guided in their writing by divine powers. Philosophically oriented minds, however, found it difficult to imagine that the rough and sometimes coarse stories of gods and men in these old poetical works were meant as they now stood. Of course it would have been deep philosophical insights which the divine inspirers had concealed in these crude forms, both the barbarous and sensual adventures of the heroes themselves and the verses in which they were described. For verses are obscure, and thus a lower form than clear philosophical treatments. Thus in Philo's setting all sorts of ways were known of discovering the actual meaning of inspired texts. Naturally for this Jew there was only one text which could be thus labelled, the Torah, breathed into Moses, the greatest of all philosophers, by the only true God himself, and under inspiration of this same God transposed into Greek.

When Moses writes, "Cain went forth from before the face of God," he cannot mean this literally. For the Self-existent Being has no face. It would then have to have a body, with internal and external organs, plus the experiences and passions which are connected with these. Besides, whither would Cain have to go in order to be away from God? God fills all that exists. "The only alternative left for us is to decide that none of these expressions is intended literally and that we must take the route of figurative interpretation which is so beloved to our philosophical minds."

After this, Philo proceeds to do with the quoted words from Scripture as is his custom: to interpret them with reference to conditions and situations of "the soul," which is not merely the principle of virtue and sin, of right and wrong, but that in man which can live in a relationship with God and therein can experience all sorts of developments. What the Torah tells about the patriarchs points to such spiritual adventures which the soul experiences in its ascent toward a mystical union with God. Thus Abraham's relocations indicate the first stage of this ascent. Relying on faith, he leaves the land of the Chaldeans behind him, that is, the world of material bodies, then in succession to leave the world of sense-perception and finally that of rational understanding. Hagar is science that is taught; his true spouse is Sarah, the knowledge of revelation. Jacob's life-course represents the second stage in this spiritual ascent. His wrestling-match is a struggle against passions. After this he receives the name of "Israel," "seer of God." The third stage is the life of Isaac, the laughing one, who has full joy. He has God as his Father, and marries the maiden Rebekah, image of the infused knowledge of God, so that he has no need of slave women and concubines, that is, of other sciences....

Where Philo, in the numerous works that are handed down to us, follows the Greek biblical text, there are all sorts of details which point him to the hidden meanings: the use of a certain preposition, the repetition of a word, the etymology of a Greek term, a word that, in strict logic, is superfluous, and so forth. Further, he has detailed speculations about the significance of biblical names, and even about the implications of numbers which appear in the text. Well known are the speculations which he bases on the fact that the creation of man is told twice. In Genesis 1:26 God makes man after his image and likeness, and in 2:7 he forms man out of clay and breathes life into him. Thus there are two men made, one a heavenly man, who according to Philo is an idea, without a body, non-sexual, by nature immortal, and the other an earthly man, the forefather of the human race.

All this may seem strange to us. Yet Philo was by no means alone in the Judaism of his time, not in his ideas and speculations and certainly not in his handling of the biblical text. The Jewish scribes in Palestine follow the same roads, using the Hebrew Torah and the two other groups of sacred books. One expert on Philo, who summarized his method of scriptural exposition in 23 rules, noted on most of them that they were also applied by the rabbis in Palestine.

About biblical exposition in Palestine in Jesus' time still

more may be said. First of all, "the tradition of the elders." In the book of the divine Torah were incorporated collections of laws that came from quite different periods. The oldest of them went back to the time before the kingship in Israel. The complex that forms the core of Deuteronomy acquired its force in the time of King Josiah, as we have seen earlier. Now with a lawbook it usually happens that customs already in vogue are accepted by the lawgiver as generally valid, and thereby acquire "the force of law." But a community is a living thing, and thus is constantly subject to change. Hence after years or centuries the need appears for a new lawbook. In view of the nature of the Torah, it was already a long way from covering, as a lawbook, all the aspects of the daily life of the Jews even when it was "canonized." There were numbers of activities and circumstances in which it was not clear to everyone what the divine lawgiver demanded of him. Then he could inquire about this from an authoritative interpreter of the Torah. Thus there arose alongside the sacred book a "tradition" of rules of conduct, a kind of oral interpretation of God's will, "Torah," which in Jesus' day enjoyed an authority equal to that of the written law. This was true at least in the circles of the Pharisees, who wanted to make the fulfilling of God's will characteristic of all the members of the Jewish nation. People liked to say of these oral explanations and expansions of the prescriptions of the Torah that they too went back to Moses himself. He had entrusted them to Joshua, who then gave them to "the oldest ones who survived him." They in turn handed them on to the prophets, and these again to "the men of the great synagogue," in the time of Ezra.

In addition to these, in some circles a very special kind of literature was developed. The canonization of the Torah and shortly thereafter of other ancient books as well was not favorable for writers who still had something to say to the Jewish community. The time of the prophets was past, according to the official position, and what the pious had to do and to allow was all fixed, from all eternity and for all time, in the Torah. But in the meantime still more disturbing things happened. Breaches were being made in the hedge which people were so carefully building about the law. In the third century B. C. Greek culture began irresistibly to penetrate the Jewish community. But now the godless Antiochus began to use brute force in order to sweep away all that the Jews had that was their own; worship and manner of life were at stake, and the law with all the hedge that surrounded it was in danger of being swept away. This was indeed the limit, the end! Formerly in such disasters God had raised up prophets to show the meaning of the events. Now men set themselves to writing, impelled by a similar spirit. Their books are called "revelation-literature," or, to use a word derived from the Greek, also "apocalyptic" books.

These writers usually chose a figure from biblical antiquity to whom God had revealed what all would happen in the future (that is, of course, in the turbulent times of the author himself) and what would happen immediately thereafter. A good candidate from biblical antiquity was Enoch, the seventh in Adam's line, who here on earth had walked with God and at the age of 365 was taken up into heaven without dying. Moses too was a suitable figure for getting a vision of the future of his people. Baruch, who had experienced the first destruction of Jerusalem and had written up the visions of Jeremiah, must himself also have received visions about the future crisis of the city. Further, it was said that a wise and equally pious Daniel had lived during the exile, at the court of Babylon. He too was a figure to whom God could have revealed something of the frightful years which his people would experience under the rage of the godless ruler, and something also of the new and eternal kingdom which he would establish immediately after these woes, for all time; and those who had died for God's good cause would have a share in that kingdom, and would shine there like stars in the heavens.

In Jesus' days a great many of this sort of "apocalyptic" books were in circulation, perhaps read in limited circles, but the expectations expressed therein lived in almost all levels of the populace. Of this varied literature only the book of Daniel attained "canonization." When the Romans in A. D. 70 destroyed Jerusalem and its temple, Judaism found new forms of life under the exclusive leadership of Pharisees. These fixed for all times the number of the sacred books at twenty-four, and rejected the apocalyptic literature. Except for Daniel, therefore, these books fell into disuse among the Jews. As a result the basic Hebrew and Aramaic texts of these were forever lost. In some Christian churches people continued to read various ones of these books, of course in translation, until they fell into disuse there also. Only in the past century have a number of the lost works again come to light in "peripheral churches," like that of Ethiopia (among others, the already mentioned book of Jubilees).

One apocalyptic book, however, continued to be read with pleasure by the Christians for centuries, in almost all churches. The author of that work represents himself as Ezra, the great father of Judaism. He has this Ezra writing in Babylon, thirty years after the first destruction of Jerusalem, thus in 557 B. C. Ezra relates seven "visions." In a way which can still be moving to a modern reader, in these he presents his questions of belief to God; about the power of evil, which he allows a free hand; and about the puzzles pertaining to his governance of the world, in which the people of his pleasure receive so little recognition.

At the end, in the seventh "vision," the author makes an effort to have his book, together with other apocalyptic works, recognized in the Jewish community, which is in the process of doing away with them. For he is writing about the year 100, about thirty years, in fact, after the first destruction of Jerusalem in the year 70 by the Romans. It may be worthwhile here to reproduce his story in brief: first of all, because for centuries the Christians regarded it as a recitation of fact, of something that the historical Ezra did in the year 557, but also because it will show how a Jewish writer from the beginning period of Christianity can conceive of "inspiration," as a consequence of his wish to provide a foundation for the authority of a writing. Ezra hears a voice saying, "Open your mouth and drink what I shall give you." He sees a cup being handed to him, with a drink which looks like water but has the color of fire. He drinks, and then feels his heart filled with knowledge, his breast with wisdom, and his mind with memory. This experience comes to him while he is voluntarily separated from the community, having taken with him only five men capable of writing rapidly. In a state of ecstasy he begins to dictate to them, and keeps this up for a full forty days and nights. He first dictates the text of the twenty-four sacred books of the Jews, which had been lost in the destruction of Jerusalem (note: that of 587!), and then seventy others besides. The first twenty-four he must make public, so that they can be read by worthy and unworthy persons alike. The other seventy (he means the "apocalyptic" ones) he may deliver only to the sages among the people.

In conclusion, something further about biblical interpretation among the "Essenes," a group of Jesus' contemporaries who had separated themselves from this evil world and all her "children of darkness," in order to await in the wilderness of the Dead Sea the great events which would put an end to the dominion of evil. These "children of light" saw their group as "the community of the new covenant." Among the finds which have been made since 1947 in the ruins of their settlement and particularly in caves in the cliffs nearby there were fragments of their biblical commentaries. In them a very specific method was followed. A couple of lines from the Bible would be given, and these would be followed by the words, "The explanation of this is...." The word regularly used here (*pesher*), evidently a technical term, appears in the second, fourth, fifth, and seventh chapters of the apocalyptic book of Daniel in our Bible. There it denotes the "exposition" of something mysterious, something that comes from God, such as the dreams of Nebuchadnezzar, the words which suddenly appear on the wall of Belshazzar's palace during a feast, and the four monster-like beasts which rise up out of the sea. Only through a kind of inspiration from God can Daniel or the angel explain what is the significance of what is seen for this present moment.

For the community by the Dead Sea this obviously is the case also with the biblical text. The text comes from God and it must have a significance for today. For this present time is the great fulfillment of history toward which all earlier centuries have looked and about which the prophets and psalmists have written in mysterious words. Central in the decisive events stands this group's own community, the chosen flock of the children of light, through whom God will destroy all the wickedness in the world. The founder of the group is referred to in the texts that have been discovered as "the Teacher of Righteousness" and is nowhere named by his own name. He must have lived in the time of the Maccabean Jonathan (160-143 B. C.) or, more likely, of Simon (143-134 B. C.). The latter must have been the "godless priest" who made it impossible for the "Teacher of Righteousness" to live in Jerusalem and drove him with his followers into the desert. The practice of interpreting the biblical texts with a view to the fortunes of his group goes back to him.

In the commentary on Habakkuk (at the end of the second verse of chapter 2) stands the following (the part printed in italics is the biblical text): "And when he says, *so that he who runs can read*, the explanation of this refers to the Teacher of Righteousness, to whom God has disclosed all the hidden things of the words of his servants the prophets. *For the vision still waits for the appointed time; but it speaks of the end and does not lie.* The explanation of this is that the end-time is protracted and all that the prophets have said is transcended. For the mysteries of God are wonderful."

The poet of Psalm 37 also continually had his eye on the

group whom we call "the Dead Sea sect," but who regarded themselves as the chosen community of the last days. They will emerge triumphant from the struggle against all evil powers, which will last for forty years. *"But those who wait for the Lord, they shall inherit the land.* The explanation of this is: they are the gathering of his elect ones, who do his will. *Yet a little while and the godless is no more; when you look for his place, then he is no more.* The explanation of this refers to all those who practice evil at the end of the forty years, who shall be destroyed, so that not a single godless person shall be found upon the earth."

The ancient texts were read by these Jews also in terms of their own believing experience, without any noticeable attention to what the biblical author in his own time had meant by his words.

5. Jesus, the Man above the Scripture

We have seen that the canonization of the Torah was connected with efforts to strengthen the Jewish sense of community. We encounter a plain formulation of that striving in the booklet of Aristeas: "Our wise lawgiver has surrounded us with unbroken hedges and with walls of iron, that we should in no way mingle with the other nations...." In Jesus' version of the Jewish religion there was no place for this segregating role of the divine book. He placed the emphasis entirely elsewhere. As the Jewish scholar Joseph Klausner put it, "his teaching became, on one hand, the negation of everything that had vitalized Judaism; and, on the other hand, it brought Judaism to such an extreme that it became, in a sense, *non-Judaism.*" The sketch that follows here is an attempt to shed some light on this penetrating statement.

a. His conduct

For years Jesus practiced the trade of carpenter in the little town of Nazareth in Galilee. Even there came the sensational report that a prophet had arisen, a certain John, who was living in the desert hills along the Jordan river. To understand why this report caused so much stir in all strata of the Jewish population, one must remember that for some centuries already people had looked in vain for prophets. In the year 167 B. C. pious Jews had uttered the lament of Psalm 74: "We do not know what all this means for us; *there are no longer any prophets!*" The Greek ruler Antiochus was then engaged in making furious efforts to impose the Hellenistic manner of life upon the Jews in Palestine, the southernmost point of his immense realm. In December of that year he not only plundered the temple in Jerusalem, for the Jews the "holy of holies," but even had sacrifices offered there to the idol which he had placed on the great altar of burnt offering. This abominable desecration was coupled with cruel persecutions, in which thousands of Jews were killed because they refused to eat pork, circumcised their children, observed the sabbath laws, and would not surrender their sacred books.

Three years after the desecration of the temple the courageous Maccabees succeeded in defeating the military force of Antiochus. From the sadly dilapidated temple they removed all traces of the pagan worship. But what must they now do with the altar of sacrifice? It had been desecrated by the abominable idol, but it still was a holy object. The decision was made to dismantle it, says the well-informed author of the first book of Maccabees, and "they laid the stones in a suitable place on the temple hill, *until a prophet should arise* who could decide what must be done with them."

The lack of prophets was, if possible, even more keenly felt at the beginning of the Christian era. Then the Romans ruled over Palestine. Herod and his sons had oppressed the people. But the direct rule by Roman governors was at least equally hateful and oppressive. Through various compromises with the occupying forces the leading priestly classes in Jerusalem tried to preserve their positions and possessions. Over against them stood the genuinely religious Jews, united in the "party" of the Pharisees. They did their best to bring as many "laymen" as possible to a strict obedience to the Torah, and thus to form an Israel that was worthy of this name, that is, a group which would be wholly and entirely guided by the will of God expressed in the law. In this way it would be evident that he ruled over them, so that one could in fact speak of a "kingdom of God" on earth. But the Pharisees achieved this only with a relatively small group, a kind of religious upper stratum, because for the ordinary man the yoke of the law was impossible to bear. He already had so many other burdens. He needed all his energies simply to get by. In addition, many wanted to live a little, genuinely to live, and that was not easy with the yoke of the law on one's shoulders. So in addition to the cleft between the worldly priests and the pious Pharisees there developed another, steadily deeper cleft between God's people who were faithful to the law and who saw themselves as "the true Israel," and the great mass of ordinary folk, identified by the pious with the old scornful term, "the people of the land." But even in this large group there were all sorts of tensions. In the year A. D. 6 the resistance movement had gone underground. In so doing it lost a few members, but it gained sympathizers time and again, whenever a harsh and hateful action of the Roman occupying forces caused the nationalist feelings to flare up. Then in addition to the groups already named there were various others, such as that of the Essenes, in their own way a "true Israel," who lived and practiced their exclusive holiness in detachment from others.

What was to become of this more and more divided and torn Israel? At the time when the Assyrians had swept over the land, God had called men like Amos and Isaiah and Micah to say to his people what the crisis had to mean. Later on, the Babylonian crisis was attended by the prophets Jeremiah and Ezekiel. But for a couple of centuries the time of the prophets seemed past and gone. What now? To know God's intentions people had nothing but texts, the Torah and the other sacred books. Texts *and* men who studied and interpreted them; scholars, only scholars. They sifted out ancient prophecies, they read books of Greek scholarship and science, and some of them wrote complicated "apocalyptic" visions; all of it ivory-tower scholarship....

Hence the sensation when the rumor made the rounds, "A prophet has arisen! Yes, a genuine prophet!" So God had finally sent someone to proclaim to his people what he had in mind with the increasingly perilous crisis. Thousands went out to see and hear the man. He was clothed like ancient Elijah, with an animal skin and a leather girdle. His message was as simple as it was demanding. The critical situation of the Jewish community signifies that God's judgment is at hand, and unavoidable. There is no escaping it, for anyone: "The axe already lies at the root of the tree." The only way to be able to survive this frightful judgment is to begin a totally new life, "repentance," as the ancient prophets had called it. Anyone who would make a firm decision to repent could demonstrate this by letting himself be immersed in the Jordan, and coming forth as a new man; this would be a break with all the sinful past.

What an experience, in this musty muddle of text and interpretation so suddenly to hear an authentic word from God, and a response in which one was so utterly and totally involved! You dip yourself in the Jordan, head and all! Naturally there came objections from the side of the orthodox. Dogma said that only heathen and sinners should succumb in God's judgment, and that the pious Jews, the true children of Abraham, would survive, to live thereafter in blessedness. The answer of the crude prophet was brief and forceful: "What are you saying? We have Abraham as our father? I say to you that God can raise up from these stones children of Abraham!" The Baptist's summons was addressed to everyone: when God comes in judgment every man is held responsible for his deeds and no one can claim any preferential place.

The carpenter from Nazareth also let himself be baptized. But he did not go back to his dwellingplace. Apparently John had opened his eyes to his own mission. He probably first joined those who were helping the Baptist, but before long he went his own way.

Like John, Jesus proclaimed that God's judgment was at hand. He too called for "repentance." Yet his preaching had a different character. He did not remain in the desert, but sought out people. The symbol of immersion, which John's converts themselves had to decide to accept, was replaced, with Jesus, by miraculous healing and liberation of those who gave credence to his words. For he spoke much, untiringly, about what concerned him. His teaching did not deal so much with the coming judgment as with the repentance which was demanded, what this should be, and where it would lead. Thus it came about that on the one hand people called Jesus a prophet, just as they had identified John, and hence as someone who did not work with biblical texts but let God's word be heard directly. On the other hand, because of his constant teaching activity, people also addressed him as "rabbi," teacher. Yet he was different from the teachers to whom people were accustomed.

Jesus did not at all give the impression of being daily occupied with the Torah and the other sacred texts. What does appear from the words which are handed down in the tradition from him is an intense interest in the people around him, and their daily lives and deeds. Particularly his parables, which are so characteristic of him, reflect numerous facets of the varied life in the houses, villages and towns of the Palestine of that day. Apparently he did not let his attention be monopolized by the study of the Scriptures, and he gave it fully and heartily to all that he saw happening around him. He spontaneously brought this experience into his teaching. His comparisons are never strained. Things that ordinarily happened among people obviously spoke to him, as pointing to the great values for which he stood.

All this has to do with the life of people in society. Jesus' interest in these relationships is evident also from his conduct. He likes to associate with all kinds of people. He is glad to be guest of well-to-do people, more, actually, than is becoming for a religious teacher. But he is equally glad to associate with the poor and the outcasts, with people whom he actually would have been supposed to avoid. Among these were, in particular, the tax-contractors, the "publicans." They had purchased from the Roman government the right to collect the indirect taxes. Men with an elastic conscience could get very rich in this way. To gain this position of course they had to have friends in the occupying forces, and that was possible only when they were not too strict in observing the divine laws about "pure and impure," which forbade commerce with the heathen. Thus the publicans, the "collaborators," were as greatly abhorred by the Pharisees as by the nationalists.

Jesus' association with them evoked sharp criticism from the side of the pious folk. He answered them no less sharply: "Those who are healthy have no need of a physician, but those who are sick." He was aware that his friendship had a healing effect. One publican in Jericho responded to his visit with the declaration, "Behold, I give half of my goods to the poor, and if I have extorted anything from anyone, I shall return it to him fourfold."

In the people whom he addressed Jesus released unsuspected powers, even in sick people who had turned to him in their despair. This despair was always in part religiously conditioned. Sickness was connected with sin and guilt. Therefore many sick people felt themselves excluded from the company of those who were in fellowship with God. Faith in Jesus appeared to have a redemptive and healing effect on them: "Your faith has made you well." He also said, "Your sins are forgiven you." It is evident that a genuine encounter with him made an entirely new beginning possible.

He asked some men from Galilee to help him in his proclamation. They entrusted their little businesses and families to others and followed him. This shows how strong a persuasive power he exerted. Yet he never used compulsion. Often he simply appealed to the sound reason and the daily experience of his listeners: "If an ox that belongs to you falls in the ditch, you do not let it lie there. . . ." Characteristic of him is a saying like the following: "Why do you yourself not judge what is right?" Sometimes he put a case before his hearers and then asked them what they thought about it. Then they were compelled to concede that he was right, not compelled by him, but by their own insight. The man who could say that he had fulfilled the two most important commandments of the law, love for God and love for his neighbor, still had one difficulty: the question remains as to what "neighbor" must be understood to mean. Is it just anybody? Jesus told him the story of the good Samaritan, a figure which in the eyes of this faithful Jew was a reprehensible man, even more contemptible than a heathen. Then Jesus asked, "Which of the three men who came along the road was, in your judgment, a neighbor to the man who had fallen into the hands of the robbers?" The man to whom Jesus addressed the question could hardly let the word "Samaritan" pass his lips, so he answered, "The one who showed mercy to the unfortunate man." Then this pious Jew had to hear that he must act according to the example of this Samaritan.

Sometimes Jesus himself was moved by the generosity which he evidently awakened. A man came to him who wanted to do anything in order to gain a share in the blessing which Jesus set in prospect, the life eternal. The great commandments, he said, he had kept ever since he was a youth. What more could he do? Jesus looked at him full of sympathy. What you can do now, he said, is to sell everything that you have, give the proceeds to the poor, and then come along with me. This appeared to the man to be too much to ask. He went away saddened. It is not related that

Jesus then made an urgent appeal to his generosity, pursued him, or threatened him. This clearly was not his way.

This is all the more striking because, as people said, he spoke with so much "authority," so utterly differently from the scribes. They brought forward texts from the Torah, and interpretations which authoritative rabbis had given of the Torah. Jesus seldom quoted the Scripture, and never did he cite the explanation of someone else. On the contrary, he explained on his own authority what God actually had intended by certain commandments and prohibitions. He evidently felt right at home with the God of Israel.

This was so evident that it was even noticed by non-Jews, such as the Roman officer in Capernaum. This man could join in a discussion of authority. He himself had sworn an oath of loyalty to the divine emperor Tiberius. It was from that fact that he drew his own authority. Thus it was that one word from him could set in motion an entire company of soldiers. He detected something of the same sort in Jesus, something like an oath of allegiance, a total submission and dedication to his God. That had to be the source from which Jesus drew the authority with which he spoke and with which he gave commands to illnesses and to demons. Jesus needed only to say one word and the illness would promptly leave the officer's tormented servant.

b. What he wanted

What did Jesus have in view? What was his teaching? To what did he summon people, so authoritatively and yet never with coercion? We have seen that for him, just as for John, God's judgment upon Israel was at hand. He too preached "repentance." But because he, in contrast to the Baptist, sought out people and associated with all sorts, he created many more possibilities to say concretely wherein this repentance must consist. Hence it is that most of the utterances which are handed down from him bear the stamp of the circumstances, of the situation into which Jesus was brought, such as encounters, questions from listeners, and criticism from opponents. There is no summary of his "doctrine" handed down, nothing that resembles a "program." For that reason it is also very difficult, if not impossible, to give in brief compass a picture of what Jesus had in view. The following is therefore nothing more than an attempt in this direction.

Perhaps one can say that Jesus strove for the formation of an Israel that would fully answer to its name and its calling, and thus that would be a genuine "people of God." But this means then God as Jesus experienced him, with whom he very intimately associated. He liked best to speak of this God as a Father, the actual Father of all men. "Your father who knows what you have need of...." "Your father who is not willing that one of these little ones should be lost...." "Your father cares for the birds that neither sow nor reap nor gather into barns...." "Your father who has numbered every hair of your head...." For Jesus God was not the strict lawgiver and judge of every outward deed, which he had been for so many Jews since the Torah had been given such a central place. He was not the concentrated holiness which was concealed in the temple, which one might not approach without the strictest precautionary measures and which one might mention in conversation only with reverent paraphrases. Therefore Jesus conceived of that genuine people of God as a brotherhood, a family, consisting of children of a Father whose sole concern and delight was to bestow gifts without discrimination, on the ungrateful and evil just as much as on the grateful and good.

What we can call the "morality" or "ethic" of Jesus then also refers exclusively to life in society. Children of his God ought to be as generous as their Father, without discrimination and without measuring out their gifts grudgingly. To give only when they expect something back in return cannot be characteristic of them; according to Jesus even "the heathen" do that. By this term he means the people who still have no idea of this Father, and who do not know that all that they are and have is pure gift. Children of God know that they live out of his mercy and forgiveness. This is why they must be ready always to forgive. "How far must I go in this? Until I forgive my brother seven times?" In order to make clear to Peter how wrong it is in this matter to ask for a measure, Jesus answers with an absurdity: "No, I say to you, you must forgive seventy times seven!"

A member of the family of this God ought to accept his fellowman without reservation. Respect for the rights of others was already, from the very beginning, included in the belief in the God of Israel. The most fundamental of these rights was this right to life: "Thou shalt not kill." Jesus demands a genuine respect for one's neighbor that goes much further: one must not allow even the first urge to eliminate someone to enter one's heart: "I say to you, anyone who is wrathful toward his brother has already made himself guilty of his death." Jesus goes to the root of the human deed. Therefore even desire for another man's wife is to be condemned as adultery. For a child of his, (Jesus') Father must be utterly transparent, with no secret places in his heart. Utterly transparent: in a certain sense this even means to be at the mercy of people. According to Jesus it is not becoming for the children of God to swear oaths. Their "yes" and "no" must be sufficient, and they are not to bring in God in order to defend themselves. Moreover, they are not to do the good works of religion in order to elevate themselves above other people. It is good to pray and to fast, but they are not to let anyone see any of this. They are to give gladly to the poor, but not to let others see this; indeed, not even to take note of it themselves. To put it in Jesus' own inimitable concreteness of expression, "Do not let your left hand know what your right hand is doing." Take part in the forms of the worship of God which are accepted in the community. But if you bring your gift to the altar and it comes to your mind that your brother has something against you, leave your gift there, go and first be reconciled to your brother, and then come back to offer your gift to God. For God is Father; one can honor him only out of a readiness to be reconciled with one's fellowmen.

All this was in line with the traditional Jewish moral teaching. But it was carried further, and thus was more radical. Jesus could — so it might be stated — hardly do otherwise, because for him God was so real: not as a lofty and holy supreme being, far removed, but as one who had a fatherly interest in people, and as the God of Israel, particularly in the crisis of the Jewish community, and in the two men whom he had sent with this crisis in view, John and Jesus himself.

Perhaps we can think here of a prophet like Isaiah in whom we can detect a similar context: an overwhelming experience of Israel's God brings with it the keen awareness that it can no longer be thus with that nation which because of its corruption, its "unbelief," no longer fits at all with the Holy One who wishes to be known as "the God of Israel." Therefore Isaiah cannot refrain from pronouncing an annihilating judgment. This is for him the real significance of the political crisis occasioned by the Assyrian invasion. But at the same time that same awareness of God makes him see that out of that "judgment" a renewed Israel shall rise, a genuine people of God, that will consist wholly of "believers."

With a great deal of caution perhaps we may presume something of the same sort with Jesus. In that case he understood that the indescribable intimacy with God was given to him in connection with the crisis in which his people found themselves. In the light of that intimacy, then, he saw more clearly than did others how bad the situation was, and at the same time he knew himself to be sent to offer the last chance for deliverance to that "Israel" that was heading toward its fall in an increasing chaos of outward violence and inward division.

It is also for this reason that Jesus stated the moral

demands of God so sharply. It was not the time to be engaged in quibbling over the commandments and prohibitions given earlier, to see just what one could do and what one could not do. The situation, biblically described as "the coming of God," demanded a radical repentance, conversion, a total commitment of the entire person. Perhaps for a time Jesus hoped to succeed in bringing all "Israel" to repentance. He called some men to help him in his proclamation of God's coming. He deliberately limited the number of these co-workers to twelve, the ancient "identifying number" of the chosen people with its twelve tribes. Thus this group was a living witness to his intention to bring together "the scattered sheep" into a new people of God that would be worthy of the name "Israel."

But Jesus quickly noted that his work was encountering resistance. The criticism by the official leaders of what he was saying and doing grew sharper in proportion as he more plainly answered them. Their objections brought him ever more sharply to formulate his message. They finally were bound to come to the decision to render Jesus harmless.

For he *was* causing trouble, in the greatest measure. Now ordinary people could indeed be enraptured at the simple and hearty manner in which he brought God near to them. But these people were not theologically schooled. They were unable to discern that in his speaking he went much too far in humanizing God. Still much worse was something else that was closely connected with this: For Jesus the Torah, the definitive and perfect revelation of God's will, came on the second level. Not that he denied or directly attacked the authority of the Torah, but he believed himself to be empowered to interpret the Torah according to his own perspective, and even in some points to criticize it, and sometimes he took no notice of the most important commandments.

For example, the law of the sabbath. The book of Jubilees, mentioned earlier, is one of the texts which testify to the inordinate reverence which this day had attained in Jesus' time. God himself observes the sabbath in heaven together with his angels. It is an exclusive prerogative of Israel to be permitted to participate in this observance. There is no clearer sign of Israel's election than the sabbath. Many Jews chose to let themselves be slaughtered rather than violating the sabbath-law by taking up arms to defend themselves. Like all pious Jews, Jesus takes part in the service in the synagogue on this holy day. But whenever he can help a person in distress, he violates the prohibition of work on the sabbath and simply declares, "The sabbath is made for man, and not man for the sabbath."

Above all, this emphasis upon *"man"*! Jesus committed the offense, and even the heresy, of associating with Jews who no longer cared about the law. Thereby they had placed themselves outside the Jewish community, outside "Israel," and thus in the same position as the mass of unclean heathen. Jesus accepted their invitations to meals. There he ate unclean foods, and naturally in his association with these people also must have committed all sorts of other ritually unclean acts. He once justified this conduct by saying, . "Nothing that goes into a person from without can make him unclean; only what comes forth from his heart can make a person unclean." Herewith he actually declared the law concerning clean and unclean foods to be invalid. The proper aim of this law was to cause the Jews to be aware of their separateness, and there he stated a principle which applied to "man." Did he then not know of the unnumbered faithful children of Israel who had let themselves be martyred rather than eat even a single piece of meat from an unclean swine?

There are a great many words handed down about Jesus which show that he often reacted very sharply to the criticism of the religious leaders. The story of the good Samaritan, which we have already mentioned, was already offensive because here Jesus had a man who stood so utterly outside Israel do something from which the pious Jew must take an example. This was already particularly nettling. But beyond this, in that story he pictured the unfortunate traveler as ignored by a priest and a Levite. This could be taken as saying, "Your religious system is lacking in mercy." He also called attention to this flaw in all sorts of circumstances. One might call to mind the pertinent brief story in which scribes brought to Jesus a woman who was taken in adultery. According to the Torah this woman should have been stoned. What does Jesus make of this? Shall he honor this judgment of the law? Or shall he, for the sake of the so-called "man," approve the sin and let this harlot go on her way? Jesus does not look up. He remains sitting, bent over, and writes with his finger in the sand. Does the case not even interest him? Or does he feel a revulsion at these triumphant pious folk who stand ready to put an end to a human life in the name of their God? As they wait, he looks up and says, "All right, enforce the law at once. But let that person among you who has never committed a sin cast the first stone." He bent over again and wrote some more in the sand. No one threw a stone. One by one the official custodians of the law left, beginning with the eldest of them. At last Jesus is alone with the woman. Then he looks at her and says, "Woman, where are they? Has no one condemned you?" The answer is, "No, no one." Then Jesus says, "Neither do I condemn you. Go, and never again be guilty of this wrong." No single act of force, not against anyone. The accusers themselves saw their own guiltiness. The woman is redeemed from her desperate situation. A new chance is given to her.

Jesus must be rendered harmless. He gives up his hope of bringing all "Israel" to repentance. The new people of God that stands before his eyes shall indeed come, but only through the "judgment" as a new life which God awakens from death. This death will consist in the destruction of the Jewish community, along with Jerusalem and the temple. But also in the destruction of Jesus himself. From the moment in which he gains a clearer awareness of all this he begins to prepare the twelve, the core-group of the new Israel, for that eventuality. The morality which he had outlined was already a radical one. Never condemn your fellowman; that gives you very little to go on in your association with others. Love your enemies; that makes life a thrilling adventure. It liberates you. Put an end to the escalation of evil by not striking back, by responding to it with good; this makes you a liberated person from the whims and crotchets of others. Forgive, ever again and again; this makes you a defenseless person. You must "deny" your entire self in order to be able to belong to the family of God that he has determined to gather around himself. All this was already radical enough. Now he begins to ask the twelve to go with him to Jerusalem. They could be certain of what would happen to him there. He was popular enough with the common people, certainly in Galilee, to be haled before the Romans as one who stirred up the people, a so-called "Messiah," a leader of the national resistance movement. Every Jew knew that the Romans made short work of such figures. For this purpose they always had crosses standing ready, which the insurrectionists themselves had to carry to the place of execution. Thus they already had hundreds of crosses standing along the roads outside the gates of Jerusalem. Now Jesus asked the twelve to be ready to go with him and as his supporters even to carry their cross to the place of martyrdom. This is how far your devotion to God must *be able* to go if you wanted to belong to the core-group of the new Israel as he had it in mind.

This was to be a society of people who did not make too much of themselves, and thus of a totally different structure from that which is customary among men. When some of the twelve showed that they would in fact like to secure for themselves a leading function in this new people of God, they learned that this indeed could be done. But then their leadership had to consist of unselfish service. No other ambition at all would fit into this new community. Jesus made this clear at a meal with the twelve, by taking upon himself the task which at a Jewish meal for guests ordinarily was performed by a slave. He washed their feet. "Who is greater, the one who sits at the table or the one who serves? Naturally, the one who sits at the table. Well, I am here among you as one who serves."

At Jesus' hearing before the High Council there appeared witnesses who accused him of the claim that he would tear down the temple in Jerusalem and then build it up again. This saying is handed down to us in various wordings. It probably goes back to a figurative saying of Jesus in which he suggests that he will replace the Jewish religion as it is practiced in his days, the "system" or "establishment," with a new form of society; the old "temple" will be replaced by a new one. Hence it is understandable that in the condemnation by the Jewish judges the word "blasphemy" appears. Jesus had laid hands on all that was holy to them, sanctified by an age-old tradition, sanctified by the blood of their martyrs, sanctified also by the seriousness of their own daily commitment. Therefore they had no other choice than definitively to remove him from their community.

6. Early Christian interpretation of the Bible

After his death Jesus appeared not only to be able to bring together the scattered group of his closest associates, but moreover to inspire them more powerfully than when he was traveling about with them. This inspiration appeared even to possess unprecedented powers to recruit others. There quickly arose, first in Palestine, then soon in Syria and Asia Minor and Egypt, communities of people who had found each other in the acceptance of Jesus as their Lord, and let their manner of thinking, hoping, and living together be determined by him. They believed that in some degree they were actualizing what he had in view in his preaching: a new family of God, one that was open to all people.

They saw all this as a "fulfillment" of the old Israel. That old Israel, in its own time, had arisen, was called together, made into a group, by a saving act of God. The common recognition of him, their deliverer, as their absolutely only Lord made Israel what it was. But the Lord remained invisible; he spoke with his people through the mediation of Moses, first of all, and then of the prophets. Finally the words given to them by God were fixed in the sacred texts, on the basis of which the Jewish community tried to find its own life. In Jesus, now, God had spoken much more directly than ever before. This man actually was not somebody who brought the message from Another. He had spoken on his own authority, and was himself, so to speak, completely wrapped up in his message. In what he had said and done and suffered he had become what he proclaimed. To put it in his own words, he had "gained his life by losing it." By so totally losing it for others, he had gained life from God in a fullness and abundance from which all mankind without distinction or discrimination could receive. The new fellowship was not based upon a written law, a letter, but upon the Lord who is alive and who gives life through the Spirit.

Of course in the first Jesus-communities a great deal was thought and said about the amazing new thing that had come upon the members. At the outset they had available, in order to be able to conceptualize and say all this, only the concepts and terms provided by Judaism. But this in itself was a great deal! The Jewish community had its wide-ranging branches in the entire known world of that time. We have already seen that their sacred books were translated into Greek, the common language in the major parts of the Roman empire. This translation naturally had contributed to the formation of an extensive Jewish-Greek vocabulary. In addition to the great Philo, whom we have already met, there were a great many other Jewish thinkers. Even in Palestine Jewish life down to the year 70 was extremely variegated. There were all sorts of groups and "sects." There, too, there was a great deal of reflection and discussion, mostly in Hebrew and Aramaic. One can assume that among the Jews in Palestine and elsewhere the level of intellectual development, as far as reading, writing, comprehension, and the capacity to formulate are concerned, was higher than among any other group in the civilized world of that day. There is no need to argue the point that this was related to the dominant role of the sacred Scriptures.

These Scriptures were equally regarded as sacred in the new communities that gathered around Jesus. The God who had expressed himself totally in Jesus was, after all, the same one who had sent Moses and the prophets and had inspired their writings. Because Jesus was the "fulfillment," the climax of this centuries-long association between God and Israel, God had caused all that earlier experience to take place and to be written down with a view to this climax. *Thus developed an entirely new interpretation of the sacred books.* As we have seen, Philo read therein his philosophical insights and mystical experiences; rabbis had tied their innumerable rules of conduct to these books; the Essenes saw the fate of their group, their founder, and his enemies portrayed therein. In exactly the same way now the Christians began to read the ancient scriptures in terms of their experiences and their faith. How Jesus had worked, what he had done and had suffered, his exaltation now to the Father's presence, his rule over the new people of God for whom he had laid the foundation, — all this was already described and pointed out by God in these Scriptures. It had all been "pre-figured." And one could likewise discern from these writings what else was about to happen now....

Of what was written and published in these first Christian communities, twenty-seven small writings are combined into the whole that we call the New Testament. They all bear witness to an intense and unwearying handling of the sacred Scriptures of the Jews. Seen thus, the New Testament is modelled after the Jewish pattern, actually a Jewish book. In the space available here we cannot even begin to portray the innumerable ways in which the Scriptures functioned therein. Just as certain definite "methods" of interpretation had already developed, every literate Christian used these together, combined them, or created new ones out of them. In addition, the ancient texts naturally were used in worship in a manner different from their use in instruction and debate, and naturally also once again in a different manner in a community of biblically loyal Jewish Christians from that among believers with a non-Jewish background. Hence in the following we offer only a few examples from the wealth of Christian interpretation of the Bible, rather arbitrarily chosen, but still with the modern reader of the Bible in mind.

a. Jesus the Messiah and the Son of God

Let us begin with a couple of texts in which many Jews saw described the Messiah whom they so ardently awaited. The term actually signifies "the anointed one." The first king, Saul, was identified in the ancient narratives with this term. David would not lift up his hand against him because he was "the anointed of the Lord." David and his successors also were all anointed ones of the Lord. After the collapse of the kingship in the destruction of the kingdom of Judah in 587 B. C., ancient expectations of a consummation of history were "messianically" colored. In the thought of many, the major figure in this consummation, the Messiah, would be a king from the house of David, who would make God's royal dominion in this world evident for all time, by representing him in a perfect government, characterized by righteousness and peace. In Jesus' time most ordinary people looked for this Messiah as the one who first of all would deliver them from the intolerable yoke of the Roman occupying forces, their Jewish collaborators, and all others who oppressed them.

At a crucial moment in Jesus' association with the group of the twelve he had asked them what they thought of him. Peter had said, "You are the Messiah." Jesus had not rejected this title, but had said that they must not call him this in public, for there were already so many people who in their grateful ecstasy wanted to urge upon him the role of national liberator. In his eyes Israel needed a more radical liberation, from much more deeply rooted evils than the Roman occupation. And he knew already at that time that he must pay for this redemptive activity with his death. The religious leaders of the Jews could not do otherwise than collaborate this one time with the priestly caste in Jerusalem, the Sadducees, and accuse Jesus to the Romans as leader of a national liberation movement, a man who pretended to be the Messiah. Pilate then also had the superscription placed on Jesus' cross to read, "the king of the Jews."

When after Easter the disciples sensed the authority of Jesus even more strongly than when he was traveling with them, it became abundantly clear to them that in Jesus God had fulfilled the ancient messianic expectations. Thus he was the one about whom David had spoken when he wrote Psalm 110:

"God said to my Lord, 'Sit at my right hand until I make your enemies your footstool.'"

With this the disciples found the expression to indicate the new position or status of Jesus: he is now exalted by God, "he sits at the right hand of God," and in this position he is addressed by David as "my Lord." Hence this formulation of the very first witnesses: Jesus of Nazareth, crucified by men, is now "installed by God to be Lord and Messiah."

A great deal was involved in this. Psalm 2 also treats of the anointed one of Israel's God. He takes up for his Messiah. Then the latter himself speaks, and says then that God has said to him:

"Thou art my son; this day I have begotten thee."

This psalm came from the court in Jerusalem. There a great deal had been adopted from the style and manner of expression which had penetrated Canaan from Egypt. There are statues which the Pharaoh had placed at the right hand of the deity which was enthroned beside him. Often his royal feet rest on a footstool on which the enemies of his country, who thus are his own enemies, are pictured. But there are also reliefs on which the deity is handing to the mother of the Pharaoh the principle of life: she "receives" her child in this way; the ruling Pharaoh is after all the son of God. Similarly the king of the pre-Israelite Jerusalem was the son of the local deity. The Israelites took over the idea, but without thinking so concretely of a begetting through the queen-mother. David was taken from following the flock and anointed to be king. His successors time and again become "son of God" at their accession to the throne. During the ceremonies they heard the repeated oracle addressed to them: "From this day forward you are my son, today I have begotten you."

This idea was expressed also by the prophet Nathan in his famous promise to David. God will see to it that a son of his own will be his successor, king of Jerusalem, and of this man God says, "I shall be to him a father, and he shall be to me a son."

Now the people of Israel as a whole was also called "son of God." An ancient story from the exodus from Egypt has Moses saying to the Pharaoh: "Thus says God the Lord: let my son depart from Egypt." The prophet Hosea used the same figure in his word from God: "Out of Egypt have I called my son," a son who according to Hosea failed to appreciate his father. Disciples of the great Isaiah placed at the beginning of their selection of his words a stout accusation which began thus: "Sons have I reared and brought up, but they have rebelled against me...."

Jeremiah, so sensitive to the fellowship-seeking character of Israel's God, translated his desire thus: "I thought, 'You shall call me "my father" and shall never leave me...'" During the test of Babylonian exile the Judeans taught that even then God should be addressed as Father: "Thou art still our Father; for Abraham has no knowledge of us, and Jacob knows us not.... But thou, Lord, art our Father, our redeemer from of old.... Thou our Father, who hast formed us out of the dust.... We all are the work of thy hands...." This was a response in prayer to the ancient naming of Israel as "son." For a Jew it was utterly impossible to conceive of any sort of physical connection in reference to this term. He could only think of a relationship of reciprocal devotion. God had given his name to this people, they were obliged only to let themselves be guided by his demands and promises, to belong to him alone, in order thus, in the midst of the nations, to be a reflection, so to speak, of God's Personhood. The writer of the Book of Wisdom, who was active in Egypt shortly before Jesus' time, pictures a pious Jew being derided by his enemies as follows: "He boasts of knowing God, and calls himself God's son.... He says that God is his father.... But if he is the righteous son of God then God will help him and will free him from those who waylay him. Therefore we shall test him, mistreat him and condemn him to a shameful death, because he will be delivered, he says, from it all...."

If Jesus' disciples were familiar with the concept "son of God" in this version, yet their Master had actualized it in a manner peculiarly his own, precisely in that aspect of total reciprocal devotion, and no less in his being the reflection of God's Personhood. In unforgettable fashion he had addressed God with the childlike, familiar "Abba." As members of the new people of God they too had to learn to pray thus to their "Abba." They could ask anything of him: "None of you would give his son a stone when he asked for bread, or a serpent when he asked for a fish! Now if being a father means this much among you, evil men, how much more will your Father in heaven give good things to those who ask him!" No listener could take exception to that "evil men" on the lips of someone who so unreservedly took their part. It issued spontaneously from the awareness that in one particular respect he stood alone. This is also evident from the "your Father." He himself lived in a relationship with God in which he could not include others. It had to be bound up with the task to which he knew himself to be destined. He was consumed by the desire to be wholly absorbed in it.

According to his own figure of speech he had to "light a fire on the earth," and he ardently longed for the time when it would blaze up. In that connection he himself would have to go through a kind of baptism: "how oppressed I feel until it shall be accomplished." This overwhelming consciousness of his mission set Jesus apart, even from his closest friends. In all his affectionate social contacts he remained at the deepest level a solitary man. Sometimes lack of understanding and stupidity made him impatient: "O, you unbelieving generation! How long must I remain with you, how long must I put up with you!" There actually was no one who really understood him, or, to put it in biblical language, who "knew" him. In a moment of elation he once spontaneously thanked his Father for his task of winning men to him. Perhaps it was on this occasion that he let it be known where he found the strength, in frightful human loneliness, to continue working: "No one knows the son except the Father."

In this connection one can also consider the above-mentioned aspect of "mirroring" (the Son resembles the Father). When Jesus was attacked because he sought out the tax-collectors and sinners and had fellowship with them at table, he told his accusers parables about the behavior of God, who goes in search of the lost and rejoices greatly when he has found them.

b. *The Scriptures in the gospels*

If he had given his disciples sufficient indications for them to recognize him fully after Easter as the expected Messiah and to proclaim him as such, and thus also as "Son" of God, the utterances just cited point to an intimacy which gave to the concept "son" a content unknown up to that time. Jesus must have belonged to God in a unique way, and must have come forth from him in the deepest conceivable sense; indeed, he must already have lived with the Father before he began his career here upon earth....

This conception also was in line with Jewish thinking. We

saw above that people expressed the absolute authority of the
Torah by saying that it existed with God before all other
things. This idea was already expressed earlier with reference
to "Wisdom." Perhaps this had arisen then out of the
awareness that Israel had developed that set of regulations
and rules for a happy life after the example of other, more
ancient peoples. In a certain sense "Wisdom" was an inter-
national phenomenon, something "universally human." It
did not belong to the unique possessions of Israel, to the
complex of election and covenant, and thus it was antecedent
to these. To state it in the Israelite fashion: it was given to
men at creation, and thus it existed with God before creation.
Therefore it could say, according to the Book of Proverbs, "I,
Wisdom, who teach you all things for a happy life, was
already born before the oceans were there.... When God
made the firmament, I was already with him...."

Thus Jesus' career did not begin with his baptism in the
Jordan, nor his life with his birth. He had lived with God, as
the only son "in the bosom of the Father." Then, after having
raised up so many men to speak his words as prophets to
Israel, God had finally sent his own son. Now the Scriptures
offered an incomparable story about a man and his only son
whom he loved. Abraham was ready to offer up his son
Isaac. He demonstrated the loftiest conceivable surrender.
Paul used the key words of that story when he wrote, "If God
is for us, who then can be against us? *He did not even spare
his own son*, but gave him up for us all. And after such a gift
will he not also give us all the rest?"

Even though Jesus himself seldom used the word "love,"
still there was no better word to identify the heart of the
entire undertaking which had issued forth from God. Out of
the many available terms which the Greek language
possessed for expressing all sorts of attachment, the Greek-
speaking church preferred to use the word *agape*, which was
rarely used in the common language. Thus this word was
filled with a specifically Christian content. John even went so

far as to indicate the mystery that is God with this term *agape*: "Everyone who loves — practices *agape* — is a child of God and knows God. The man without this love does not know God, for God *is* love (*agape*). And the love which God is has been revealed among us by his sending his only son into the world in order to bring life."

Thus in the eyes of his disciples Jesus had a "pre-history" in eternity. It is true that only after his death did he become for them the Lord in the most absolute sense of that word. But upon deeper reflection it appeared to them that this "post-history" had to be matched by a "pre-history," a glory which Jesus possessed with the Father before the foundation of the world; thus they saw his as a life in three phases. The middle phase was that of the humiliation; he had "emptied" himself by assuming the form of a ministering man and becoming obedient even to death on the cross.

It is good to think of all this upon reading the gospels. The writers tell something about the conduct, the suffering and the death of Jesus, this middle phase, but all through this runs their belief in the pre- and post-history, which they had discovered when they began to read the Scriptures in the light of their overwhelming experiences with him.

Because he "fulfilled" the Scriptures, those who told about Jesus' life found there all sorts of material that more or less heavily influenced the form of their narratives. So even if it were possible systematically to describe that use of the Jewish Scriptures in the gospels, that would require a thick book. So here only a couple of examples to give an idea of that use of the Scriptures.

Most biblical, of course, were the narratives surrounding Jesus' birth. As is usual with figures of great historical significance, that beginning point of his life came to be a matter of interest only many years after his death, this as a starting point for legends which aimed at expressing the significance and the characteristics of his person. Jesus came from Nazareth. People had identified him by that place, as Jesus of

Nazareth or the Nazarene. But as the Messiah he had to be a descendant of David, and born in Bethlehem as well, for the prophet Micah had predicted this. Luke's account has his parents go to Bethlehem just before his birth, because of a census which the emperor Augustus is said to have decreed. Matthew's account simply has Jesus born in Bethlehem, and has him later moved to Galilee upon instructions given by God, to Nazareth, because according to "prophetic" texts (not clearly identified by Matthew) he was "to be called a Nazorean."

Joseph receives the instruction to go to Galilee in a dream, the fourth revelatory dream in the story. His ancient namesake in the book of Genesis was also a person who received insights and instructions in dreams and therefore was called "the dreamer." Both evangelists employ a genealogy to show that Jesus was a descendant of David. For this too belonged to the concept of the Messiah. One could not conceive of the Messiah differently. Just how the genealogies were constructed therefore did not matter very much: Matthew gives different names between David and Joseph from those given by Luke.

The prophecy of Micah which identified Bethlehem as the birthplace of the future ruler over Israel spoke further in enigmatic words about "his origin in the days of eternity," and rather mysteriously referred to his mother as "she who shall give birth." Something of the same sort was to be found in the book of Isaiah. The unbelieving king Ahaz was given a sign: "The woman is pregnant with a son who shall be called *Immanuel,* God-with-us." The Greek translation had emphasized the mysterious character of the pregnancy by translating the word "woman" as "virgin." Thus arose the story that the mother of Jesus had conceived him directly through the action of God, without the medium of a man.

For such a working of God the Scriptures offered a set term: the wind, storm-wind, or breath of God, in the Hebrew language the *ruach* of God. In our Bibles and in the language

of the church this word is always translated as "Spirit" of
God. Therefore we no longer sense so directly that with this
word the biblical men were reminded of blowing or
breathing. People in antiquity found these phenomena
mysterious. The wind can come with great power without
our having ever seen it, and thus it is an expressive symbol
for God; and the breath is an unmistakable sign of the
mysterious life-force which works in man and animal alike.
Hence people liked to speak of the wind or the breath of
Israel's God (in our Bibles the "Spirit" of God) where he had
"stormily" intervened, where he had stirred men to surpass
themselves and to become great deliverers of his people — his
"Spirit" had made different men of them — or where he
caused prophets to speak powerfully to his people. After the
Exile people also attributed to this *ruach* of God, or to the
"Holy Spirit," the hoped-for re-creation of the human heart
that is hardened in unbelief. After Easter the disciples of Jesus
sensed that they had become different people, and this
awareness of an entirely new beginning they imparted to all
who accepted this Jesus as their Lord and who thereby
became members of the group which he gathered about
himself, the new people of God, his "church" or his *corps*,
which means "body." All members shared in this inspiration.
This too was predicted by a prophet. According to Joel, at
the consummation of history God would "pour out his *ruach*
upon all mankind, upon men and women, upon old and
young, upon masters and servants...." Now they were
experiencing the fulfillment of these words. Only it appeared
that this mighty re-creating power of God had issued from
Jesus. In him the powerful *ruach* had first been concentrated.
He himself had rarely spoken about this Spirit of God. It was
the narrators who introduced the Spirit into the narratives
about him, as for example in that of his baptism in the
Jordan. And those who told of his birth from the virgin
explicitly attributed his being begotten to the Holy Spirit.

Luke has Jesus' birth first announced to shepherds. While

most of the details of his sensitive chapters about the beginning of Jesus' life are borrowed from the Scriptures, and are formed according to the model of biblical narratives, these shepherds appear rather to be inspired by what Luke most admired in Jesus' conduct: his preference for despised and outcast people. Apparently he knew that the middleclass milieu of Jerusalem had no use for shepherds, those unclean people from the desert, as impudent as they were untrustworthy, whom one would call "sinners." Therefore Luke has the good news of the Messiah first announced to them. Matthew also lets himself be guided in his telling of the story by a later situation. In his community people were constantly amazed at the fact that the leaders of the Jewish community rejected Jesus, while the non-Jews in steadily increasing numbers accepted him as their Lord, to whom they gave the best of themselves. Therefore Matthew has Gentiles come from the East, who had their attention drawn by a star (this happens in several Jewish stories) to the birth of the Messiah. A great many of the biblical texts told of the wisdom of the easterners. Astronomy also came from these eastern lands. With all their learning, these men still do not know where they must look for the newborn Messiah. That is known only by the Jews themselves, who possess the Scriptures, the prophecies. The chief priests and scribes then also tell what is given to them to know: The Messiah is born in Bethlehem. They themselves, however, do not go to worship him. The heathen wise men do this, and they bring him gifts such as are described beforehand by the Scriptures such as Psalm 72 and Isaiah 60. In the latter text the gifts are brought by the heathen to "Zion"; this stands for the chosen people who are once again accepted by God in grace, and who represent, "reflect" him on this earth. But the Messiah does this in a much more intensive and definitive way.

This motif also figures in the sequel to Matthew's narrative. In Jesus' career the fate of Israel is, so to speak, recapitulated. Thus Matthew has Jesus' parents flee with their child to Egypt. Joseph receives the command to do this in a dream. In this way he can make true the statement of Hosea which we have already cited: "Out of Egypt I have called my son."

But as leader of the new people of God Jesus also "fulfills" the figure of Moses. The book of Exodus begins by telling how Moses as an infant was saved from a general slaughter of the children, by God's providence. Matthew now has king Herod play the role of the murderer. He can relate to this the word of Jeremiah about the weeping of Rachel over her children, because in his time the grave of Rachel was thought to be located near Bethlehem.

In biblical thought the concept of "servant" is very closely related to that of "son." The life of the devoted servant is wholly determined by the task and the wishes of his master. One can, as it were, infer the personality of the master from what his faithful servant does and allows. Israel is characterized by the fact that she serves this one God and recognizes no other power over her, or at least is not permitted to recognize any such. Various individual "servants" appear to spur her on to the exclusive service of her God. The lives of Moses and of so many prophets after him were wholly determined by their task of making Israel wholly committed to the service of her God. In the second part of the book of Isaiah such a servant repeatedly appears, utterly devoted to God, and God to him. Sometimes he appears to be a personification of Israel; more often he is clearly an individual who has a task to fulfill for that nation, and this in such a way that other nations also are affected thereby. Then he appears to sum up in his person the devotion and the submissiveness of Moses and Jeremiah and the other prophets. This "ideal" servant continues to fulfill his task with respect to rebellious Israel to the bitter end. To the astonishment of the other nations he is slain as a sin-offering for the sins of all and thereafter God bestows upon him an abundance of life. So he can "make righteous" unnumbered multitudes, that is to say, can bring them into a communion of life with his God.

It cannot be determined with certainty whether Jesus himself thought of his task in the light of Isaiah's ideal servant. It does appear from the entire New Testament that his disciples did think of it thus, in all sorts of ways. In this connection we may be reminded that many Jesus-groups speedily emerged in Greek-speaking settings, where people used the Greek translation of the Jewish Scriptures. In this language the word *pais* could signify both servant and son.

The story of Jesus' baptism in the Jordan has a voice sound from heaven, which appears to combine two biblical texts: the words addressed to the Messiah in Psalm 2, "You are my son," and those in Isaiah 42 with which God presents his servant, "Behold my servant in whom I am well pleased." We have already seen that it was the summons of John that had drawn Jesus from Nazareth. Perhaps it was at his baptism that a first glimpse of his task was granted to him. In any case, his disciples later saw in his baptism the decisive moment; one could say, the moment of his "call." But this then is not as in the case of the prophets, who only at the moment of their call receive their function and are installed as prophets. For in Jesus' case, the author has the heavenly voice (or the "inspired" words of Scripture) only confirm who he *is* already. It is true that the descent of the Spirit in the form of a dove points to the conviction that Jesus then began with his life-awakening activity.

What follows then has Jesus remaining in the wilderness for forty days, just as Israel after passing through the waters of the Red Sea remained forty years in the wilderness. Like Israel, in this situation Jesus was put to the test. This motif clearly has played a part in the formation of the story; one should only read Deuteronomy 8 alongside this. But it shows Jesus face to face with Satan, the great adversary of God and man. Satan offers him suggestions which coincide with the temptations to which Jesus was exposed during his active ministry: concern for himself, success through spectacular miracles, and the urge to rule. It may be that his disciples have later collected and combined these in this "beginning narrative." It is possible that there remains here as a kernel of the story a naturally symbolic indication from Jesus himself, explaining how after his baptism he had "bound the strong man," by setting his own firm determination over against other possibilities which were set before him to entice him.

Among the miracle stories in the gospels, some are strongly pervaded with motifs from the Jewish Scriptures. Jesus was "the fulfillment" of them. Thus it was told there that Moses had fed his people in the wilderness with miraculous food, the manna. It was also told how the prophet Elisha, with a couple of loaves of bread, had fed a hundred men so royally that there was some left over. In the Jesus-communities a story circulated about a feeding of some thousands of men who had followed him into the desert, an evident "fulfilling." The evangelist Mark already knew at least two versions of this story which he incorporated into his book. In both cases, the manner in which Jesus takes the bread, blesses it, and distributes it is reminiscent of his action at the Supper, which was repeated by the Christians weekly. This repeatedly experienced miraculous feeding also had an influence upon the form of the story.

More than once Jesus had referred to the figure of Jonah and the inhabitants of Nineveh, who at his preaching had at once been converted. The brief story about the fate of Jonah was generally known. It probably played a part in what people told about the storm on the sea. In the story, Jonah fled from his assigned task, and took a boat to Tarshish, in the exactly opposite direction from Nineveh. Then there arose such a fierce storm that the ship threatened to be lost. But Jonah did not notice anything. He was fast asleep in the boat. So also Jesus slept peacefully in the stern of the boat that was about to sink, with disciples and all, in a sudden violent storm. But Jesus was a "fulfillment" of Jonah, in the sense that he was obedient to God and therefore could sovereignly command illnesses and demons and all the forces of nature. For those who first told the story the boat was a figure of the church, which in threatening peril prayed as did the biblical believers, "Awake, O Lord!"

Many biblical motifs are evident in the so-called "transfiguration." It takes place on a high mountain which is not identified by name. It could not be named, because what was meant by this was a mountain which did not lie in Palestine, the "mount of God," where the great revelations took place: there Moses and Elijah were permitted to see something of the divine glory. There Jesus' face suddenly becomes radiant, and his clothing becomes luminous. He is dazzling, like the heavenly figures who appear in some biblical books, for example those in Dan. 10. Then come the two men whom people expected to see on the mount of God, Moses and Elijah; that is, the Law and the Prophets. Jesus begins to talk with them. In those books, the Law and the Prophets, indeed, was written what the Messiah must suffer in order to be able to enter into his glory. Luke, who so strongly emphasizes this point, explains the story by relating that Jesus' conversation with them concerned "his exodus which he would accomplish in Jerusalem." Then appears the cloud, the customary biblical symbol of the presence of God. From the cloud a voice utters the same biblical texts which were pronounced at the baptism in the Jordan, and then adds a word from Moses. In Deut. 18 Moses prophesies that God will raise up a prophet after him, and then he commands, "You must listen to him."

Finally, the stories about Jesus' suffering and death. In these, texts and motifs from the Scriptures are quickly interwoven with the reminiscences of eyewitnesses. In some psalms the speaker is a believer who prays, out of a gravely imperilled situation; illnesses, blows, and enemies conspire against his life; then his prayer suddenly turns into a song of praise to his God who has heard his prayer and has rescued him out of the clutches of the "underworld." He begins to offer a thank-offering, *eucharistia*, for the new life that God has given him, and he invites all true seekers after God to join him in it. In the psalms of this kind "David" obviously had not spoken in his own name, but was prophetically describing the fate of his distant descendant, the Messiah, just as Isaiah had done in his utterances about the ideal servant of the Lord.

The one uttering the prayer in Psalm 22, "My God, my God, why hast thou forsaken me?", describes how his enemies ridicule him after they have pierced his hands and feet. Moreover, "they divide my garments among them, and cast lots for my raiment."

The speaker in Psalm 69 has become a stranger to his brethren because "zeal for thy house, O God, has consumed me." His enemies have given him poisonous food and "in my thirst they gave me vinegar to drink."

In chapters 9-14 of the book of Zechariah, the Christians found a mysterious prophecy of what would happen in the days of the consummation. The passage began with a summons to Jerusalem to welcome her king with rejoicing. He comes "righteous and triumphant, humble and riding on an ass, and proclaiming peace to all the nations of the earth." A little later it speaks of "a flock without a shepherd." This theme then leads to the image of a shepherd who gets his wages in the form of "thirty pieces of silver." At God's command then he throws that money, the usual price of a slave, "before the potter in the temple." Just after this, the prophecy deals with the inhabitants of Jerusalem, who "shall look on him whom they have pierced," and about whom they raise a lament "as over an only son." Presently the theme of the shepherd returns; the shepherd is smitten, "so that the sheep are scattered." The closing sentence of Zechariah's obscure prophecy is formed by the prediction that "on that day there shall no longer be any trader in the temple of Israel's God."

This latter point was clearly fulfilled by Jesus when he drove the moneychangers and merchants out of the temple, while he had made the former part come true when he rode into Jerusalem on an ass. Thus there was every reason to use other details of Zechariah's prophecy in the accounts of these crucial events.

The climax of these events was Jesus' death. It concluded the entire pre-history and opened the new, final, definitive era. Before long people were telling that at the very same moment the curtain of the temple was rent from top to bottom, a significant symbol: God was now no longer concealed and inaccessible, the old temple had served its purpose.... Very soon people also introduced impressive natural phenomena. Coupled with the eclipse which Luke describes, an earthquake appears in Matthew, so powerful that it splits the rocks. This phenomenon also comes from the Scriptures. Many ancient biblical texts represent nature as reacting to an intervention of Israel's God. It will do this on the great day of the end also. Thus Amos prophesied: "On that day it will come to pass that I shall cause the sun to go down at midday, and in broad daylight shall place the land in darkness." Perhaps the attention of the Christians was drawn to this text because immediately after this he speaks of the "mourning for an only son."

Even from these few scattered examples one can gather something of the nature of the four gospels. They preserve recollections of Jesus' person and conduct, but these then are set in a biblical frame, a biblical context. Perhaps a better comparison would that of a woven canvas: recollections of what he has done, said, and suffered are intertwined, sometimes inextricably, with what *must* have happened there because he "fulfilled" the old Scriptures. To put it in another way: people were describing *at one and the same time* the enigmatic and appealing person with whom they had been associated *and* the Son of God who he appeared to be in the light of the Easter experiences, the Messiah who was announced and described in so many biblical texts.

c. The Scriptures in the letters of the apostles

We have begun with the use of the Bible in the gospels,

because many are most familiar with them. But we possess still other testimonies to that use of the Scriptures in the epistles of Paul. Let us see, on the basis of a few examples, how he used the old Scriptures in thinking through, defending, and formulating his new faith.

Paul had received his religious instruction at the feet of the famous rabbi Gamaliel. He stood out above his fellow-pupils in his zeal for the Torah and the traditions of the fathers. Thus he became familiar with the many ways in which the Pharisees' insights of belief, their patterns of life, their views of God and man, of salvation and perdition, were based on the Scriptures. Hence it is that Paul vigorously went to war against the people who worshipped the Messiah in the crucified Jesus of Nazareth. Paul had heard enough of him to see that he was the opposite of a Messiah. For he had undermined the principles of the Jewish community. One could see this clearly in this pack of followers: almost all of them were people who did not live according to the Law, "fringe-church people." And they were to be the people of the Messiah! What was still worse was that this heresy was spreading like an epidemic. Even Jewish communities outside Palestine were already being affected by it.

As radical as was Paul's fight against this heretical business, his commitment to it was equally vigorous, after he was struck by the new view of Jesus as by a bolt of lightning. He immediately saw, more clearly than many disciples of the first hour, the dimensions of the new people of God that Jesus had in view. He had included therein all who could not bear the yoke of the Law, all who were officially excluded from salvation. But then this great mass of those excluded, who in the Jewish terminology were called the nations, *goyim*, "heathen," must also be included in the people of God.

As the crucified one Jesus was, according to the law, a person accursed: "Cursed be he who hangs on a tree." If he was installed by God as the Messiah, then God had therewith rendered his law invalid. Then all who on the basis of the law were accursed could be incorporated into the people of this Messiah.

Years later, looking back on this reversal in his life, and thinking of his youthful zeal for the law, and how he had persecuted the Christians, Paul wrote: "But then God, who had chosen me from the time of my birth and called me by his grace, determined to reveal his Son to me, that I should proclaim him among the Gentiles." He had received that new vision of Jesus as a commission. It surely is not accidental that he begins the sentence just quoted with an expression of the servant of God in Isaiah 49:

"You coastlands, listen to me;

Listen attentively, you distant peoples:

The Lord has called me from the moment of my birth...."

For Paul could not help thinking of this totally new thing that had come to him in the light of the Scriptures. And thus he formulated his task in the words of the servant in Isaiah, who was destined to cause God's salvation to reach to the ends of the earth.

But Paul also suddenly discovered the universal note in all sorts of other biblical texts. Thus in various psalms David had spoken about the heathen nations who should come to praise God, and sometimes he expressly summoned them to do so. The fulfillment of this was now in process, and Paul was granted the privilege of sharing in this work.

But it still remained difficult for many Jews who accepted Jesus as the Messiah to follow Paul. That Gentiles were incorporated into the Messianic nation without any formality was difficult for them to assimilate. For many generations it had been impressed upon them that one must be circumcised in order to belong to that people, that one must abstain from unclean foods, in short, that one must fulfill the major commandments of the Law. One must do something in order to become a partaker in the salvation of the Messiah. Was not Paul making access to it altogether too easy?

In his discussions with these Christians Paul always used his Bible which he read, with them, in the Greek translation. Best known is his handling of all sorts of details in the story of Abraham.

The book of Genesis describes (in chapter 17) how Abraham received from God the commandment to circumcise himself and all his male descendants; this was the sign of their special bond with God, the sign of their "election." But Paul points out that already earlier in the narrative in Genesis (chapter 15) God had formed this covenant with Abraham, and Abraham had believed his promise of offspring. This faith made Abraham righteous in God's eyes. Thus it stands in the text of Genesis. Now, Paul remarks, Abraham was not yet circumcised at that time. In this quality, then, as uncircumcised, he could become "father" of the Gentiles who now are entering the company of the people of God, just as well as the Jews who do this in the same faith, and therein do not appeal to their circumcision. Thus Abraham could become the father of many nations.

Paul goes still further. That faith of Abraham did not differ in essence from that of the Christians. For the story in Genesis says that Abraham was a hundred years old when a son was promised to him, at a time when the womb of his aged Sara was already long since "dead." Yet he trusted that God would fulfill this promise. This was thus a surrender to him who awakens life out of death. Well, now, that is precisely the kernel of the new faith: surrender to the God who has awakened the crucified one to life and made him the central figure of the new people of God who participate in his new life with God. Or, better said, in the new family of God. For, altogether in line with Jesus, Paul says that all people receive a share in "the sonship" that belongs to Christ by nature. And this includes everything. After all, a son inherits the possessions of his father; thus through their faith the Christians are "fellow-heirs."

Sometimes Paul's use of biblical texts reminds us of Philo.

The Greek text of Genesis says that the promise is given to Abraham "and to his seed." Now Paul says that it does not have a plural form, "to his seeds," but a singular. Thus the text refers to Christ! To us this appears a bit of rather artificial interpretation, "eisegesis" rather than exegesis, all the more since Paul was familiar with the Hebrew text and knew that the word for "seed" used here has a collective significance, meaning "posterity, progeny." But this interpretation, or eisegesis, is placed entirely at the service of his train of thought, which indeed is entirely sensible. For here he sees the promise to Abraham as a sort of testament of God. Now according to the Greek text of the book of Exodus, the Law came 430 years later than that testament. It could not annul the promise that was made therein; thus it had another function, which necessarily ceased when the promise was fulfilled in the "seed," Christ, the heir.

If one knows how to read the Law aright, one sees the new salvation everywhere indicated, and even the situations in which it is now being actualized. Paul can understand that the Jews remain bound to the Law; they consider themselves bound to circumcision and all the other usages which make them unfree in relation to others; all their customs have precisely the aim of hindering their communication with others. Moreover, they annoy the Christians because the latter regard the totality of these usages which isolate and disrupt communication as outmoded and superfluous. This situation also is indicated in the Scriptures. There, too, we can find an unfree figure who is an annoyance to a free one. It is told of Abraham that he begot a son, Ishmael, by his slavegirl, Hagar. When this slave-son annoyed his half-brother Isaac, he was sent into the desert with his mother. Ishmael, son of the unfree woman, should not be allowed to share in the inheritance of Abraham with Isaac, the son whom God had given, by virtue of his promise, to Sara, the free woman. Parenthetically, Paul says that Ishmael — as is known, the ancestral father of the Arab peoples — was sent into the Arabian desert; it is not accidental that that is precisely where Sinai lies, the mountain where the Law was given. The Jews of the present, slaves of the Law, are indicated by this Hagar, the slave girl, mother of the likewise unfree son. We Christians are Isaac, children of the promise, who belong to another Jerusalem, so different from this earthly city in which unfree Judaism has its center....

"You must not muzzle an ox that threshes the grain." This stands in the Law. For us modern men it bears witness to the spirit of the book of Deuteronomy, which often prescribes a humane treatment of animals. But for Paul, and for all Jewish and Christian readers in antiquity, this is a word from God, mediated to his people through Moses. Paul can hardly imagine that God is concerned here with animals. Naturally he is concerned for men, and in the light of Christ this must refer to the new situation. For everything was surely written "for the sake of us who are experiencing the fulfilling of the times." The aim of this word from God must be this: the person who devotes all his time to providing spiritual food for the Christians has a right to support from them for his physical needs.

These are only some examples of the highly varied use of the Bible which we encounter in Paul's own epistles. In the other writings of the New Testament the use of the Bible is equally varied. It is extraordinarily elaborate in the letter to the Hebrews, a profound message of encouragement to Christians who have come out of Judaism, who have to suffer at the hands of their former companions, and who are so discouraged that they harbor some homesickness for the majestic ceremonies in the temple at Jerusalem of which they were so fond. The writer of this document, which is cast in very excellent Greek, must have reflected for many years upon the ancient Scriptures in the light of the new faith. With great skill he uses all the methods of interpretation cherished by the Jews, in order to show how in Christ, the Son of God and the true High Priest, Israel's ancient worship is completely "fulfilled."

Interesting for our theme is an example of biblical interpretation in the epistle of James. This writer finds mere faith, without "works," a dangerous thing. One can very well believe that there is one God, but so do the devils. "Do you want proof that faith without works is vain? Was not our father Abraham justified because he placed his son Isaac on the altar as a sacrifice? You see that his faith accompanied his works, and only became perfect through these works." Thus was the Scripture fulfilled which says, "Abraham believed and it was reckoned to him for righteousness." At first glance this appears to be a polemic against Paul; both of them use the same biblical texts.

In the same connection James also cites the case of Rahab the harlot. According to the book of Joshua she was justified on the basis of her works: she had hidden the spies in her house and had helped them escape from Jericho. Later on we shall meet Rahab again, because of her Christian career, which begins here with James.

7. The new Bible and the church fathers

Very difficult to define, and therefore giving occasion to much misunderstanding, are the biblical concepts "spirit" and "spiritual." We have spoken earlier of the Hebrew term "ruach" and the Greek word "pneuma." To people of the Bible these words meant wind and breath, and the stormlike events in which they detected the dynamic presence of God.

In our minds, the word "spiritual" always evokes the idea of something non-material, incorporeal, whether with or without other nuances such as "higher" or "inward": a person's inner life is hidden, in contrast to his outward conduct. But this is not what the people of the Bible meant. When Luke sums up the spiritual experiences of the first disciples in an event which he has taking place on Pentecost, he brings into the picture (in a thoroughly biblical way) "a rushing sound as of a powerful wind" and "tongues as of fire," which cause the disciples to burst forth in an enthusiastic testimony. In addition, Luke notes what kind of impression this spiritual experience of the Christians made on the outsiders: "these men are drunk."

Thus this working of the Spirit is spectacular. But this does not mean that it is any less inward. One must even say that the working of the Spirit becomes visible *because* he has penetrated to the deepest level of the human heart. This Spirit has destroyed the last bulwarks behind which self-centeredness strives still to fortify itself. Thereby he has broken man open, and redeemed him from his state of isolation. Then man has become open to all others. With Jesus he can speak to God as "Abba," and can greet his fellowmen as brothers. The bond that joins him to them is intense, because it has very deep roots. Therefore this group can also be called "the temple of the Holy Spirit" as well as "the body of Christ."

When the Christians of this first period speak of a "spiritual" reading of the Jewish Bible, they mean a relating of the ancient texts to what they are now experiencing in this new community of which Jesus is the living center. In the preceding section we saw a couple of examples of this new, "spiritual" interpretation. Not included among those is a well-known passage from Paul's second letter to the Corinthians. Paul points out that because of their refusal to recognize Jesus as the Messiah, the Jews cannot understand the real meaning of their Holy Scriptures. After he has spoken in rabbinical fashion — and thus for us in rather complicated fashion — about the veil which Moses had to put over his face, according to the story in Exodus 34, he writes: "Their minds were hardened. In fact, down to the present day the same veil has remained when they read the Old Testament. It is not removed, because Christ alone causes it to disappear. To this day a veil lies over their minds, whenever Moses is read. But when anyone turns to the Lord, the veil is removed. Now the Lord is the Spirit, and where the Spirit of the Lord is, there is liberty."

Here Paul is speaking about things with which his thought

and contemplation were constantly engaged. Among these things was the utterly new experience which he within himself, and his fellow Christians, continued to have, as well as the other side of the coin, which troubled him: so many Jews for whom this new experience is not available. They remain closed to the real, "ultimate" meaning of the Holy Scriptures which God has given to them.

For the Christians the old Bible has actually become a new book, through this "spiritual" understanding. But in the following centuries there arises still another reason to speak of a "new Bible." In the course of a process the details of which are difficult to survey, a number of writings from the circle of the Christians of the first century acquired the same rank as the Jewish Bible. They were regarded as inspired in the same sense. So there came into being the whole collection which presently was to be called the Bible (by way of the Greek *biblos*, "book," in the diminutive form also *biblion*, and the Latin *biblia*), *the* book *par excellence*.

The twenty-seven writings which were added to the Jewish sacred books were indeed called "the New Testament," but to the Christians' mind they formed an organic whole with what they began to call the Old Testament. This was true primarily because they bore witness to the Christian salvation in images and terms which almost without exception were borrowed from the Jewish writings. But it was also because these too were "spiritually" interpreted. For the new reality in which the Christians lived was indeed on the one hand a "fulfilling" of what had happened and was written before Christ, but on the other hand it also still was open to a further fulfillment. Paul had already said this in his inimitable way which will never disappear from Christian memory: "Our knowledge (of God's secrets) is only partial." These ultimate things which God has prepared for those who love him we now see "as in a blurred mirror" in comparison with the perfect fellowship in Christ which God will ultimately give us and in which we shall see him "face to face." Therefore the life of Christians together here has the characteristics of childishness, of immaturity. Even the most sublime utterance among ourselves is only a stammering. Whatever we attempt to express about salvation is always only a kind of signpost, an indicator pointing in the direction of the reality. This even holds true of the manner in which this is done in the New Testament, even in the most prominent books there, the gospels. What Christ does and says and suffers there has a dimension which escapes the superficial, "non-spiritual" reader. For him it is nothing but an account of events which forever belong to the past. Only the person who relates them to what he is experiencing now as a member of the church on the way to fulfillment, that is, one who reads them "spiritually," understands the intention with which God is speaking to him here and now through the texts.

In order to make this somewhat more concrete for the modern reader, and less disconcerting as well, let me relate a couple of expositions of the Bible from some church fathers. I shall begin with *Origen*, who has had more influence on the Christian interpretation of the Bible than any other church father.

Born about the year A. D. 185, he received his first schooling in Alexandria from his father Leonidas, who shortly after the year 200 paid for his Christian faith with a martyr's death. After some years of university studies, Origen was charged by the bishop of Alexandria with the task of instructing new converts to the faith, the catechumens. After he had handed over this task to his pupil Heracles, he was able to devote himself more to his studies and to study tours which took him to Rome as well as to Palestine and Arabia. About A. D. 230, as a result of difficulties in Alexandria, he moved to Caesarea, on the coast of Palestine, then a flourishing center of Christian life. There too he devoted himself untiringly to the study of Christianity, on the basis of an insatiable association with the Bible, from which he also preached almost daily for many years.

This much-traveled theologian knew almost everything that went on there in his time, with the Christians themselves and in their contacts with Jews and pagans. Through his own perceptive and reflective mind this wealth came to rest in his innumerable writings. Unfortunately many of those writings have been lost. For Origen was compelled to be original on all sorts of points of Christian thought. He was called upon to give answers to questions which had never before been posed thus, and to which therefore no thought-out and accepted answers were available. Thus it came about that in the following centuries he became the subject of vigorous theological disputes. Therefore also many of his writings were, so to speak, taken out of circulation and no longer copied. It is fortunate that a number of his expositions of the Bible were translated into Latin as early as the fourth century. They enjoyed great esteem in the western church. Hence people continued to copy the texts through the centuries, and thus it happened that his influence was decisive for the Latin-speaking church. One expert in the field has said, "To write a history of Origen's influence on the west would be tantamount to writing a history of western exegesis."

Origen preaches on Exodus 2: the daughter of Pharaoh has found a child in a basket made of bulrushes, has him brought up, takes him into her palace, and gives him the name of Moses.

"Every word of this text contains a boundless mystery. It would require a great deal of time to expound this, and if we wished to draw out everything that is in it, an entire day would not be sufficient. But let us try to say something about it briefly, for the edification of this gathering. I think that one can see in Pharaoh's daughter the image of the church, which is assembled out of the heathen nations. Although her father is evil and godless, it is said to her from the mouth of the prophet: 'Listen, my daughter, consider and incline your ear; forget your people and your father's house, for the king is captivated by your beauty.' Thus she leaves the house of her father and goes to the water in order to wash away the sins which she has committed in her paternal home. Then she is immediately moved by feelings of compassion and takes pity on the child. Thus this church which comes from the heathen finds Moses alongside a shore, Moses who is rejected by his own people and left as a foundling; she has him brought up in his own milieu, where he spends his childhood. When he is grown, he is brought to her and then she takes him to be her son. We have already often explained that Moses signifies the Law. Thus also the church, when she comes to the waters of baptism, receives the Law which lay hidden there in a basket that was covered with pitch and tar. The Law was enclosed in a wrapping like that; it was covered with pitch and tar, entangled in the cheap and earthly interpretations of the Jews, until the church of the nations came to take her out of the muck and mire of the swamps and to give her a place in the royal courts and palaces of Wisdom. Nevertheless the Law spent her childhood in her own milieu. It is true that among those who are incapable of understanding her spiritually she is very small, a child that is fed with milk that is for children. But when she comes to the church and enters into that house, she becomes a Moses who is strong and robust. When one has once thrown away the veil which is the letter, then one finds in the reading of the law a food that is substantial and perfect."

One of the noteworthy things in this suggestive text is the interweaving of the figures of Moses and the Law which was written by him. Origen shared in the great veneration for the figure of Moses which was and is so characteristic of the Jewish tradition, particularly in Alexandria, where Philo had lived. Among all the favored figures of the Old Testament Moses was the most highly favored, in Origen's eyes as well. While David and Isaiah had received a very clear vision of the incarnate Son of God whom they announced, Moses had had a more intimate association with him than any other man, and fully comprehended the deepest spiritual meaning of the laws and stories which he wrote down. To him and all these others the light was given, in advance, which would become manifest in Christ. They borrowed their brilliance from him; the actual meaning of their writings becomes clear only in his light. Hence it is that the story of Jesus' transfiguration on the mountain appears so frequently in Origen's sermons and discussions. Thus in one place he writes:

"If anyone has seen and beheld the Son of God when his visage is altered so that his appearance is like the sun and his clothing like the light, then Moses (that is, the Law) suddenly appears to him, and in Moses' company Elijah as well; not these alone, but there also appear to him all the prophets, in conversation with Jesus. If anyone in this manner has seen the glory of Moses by beholding the spiritual Law as a word that refers altogether to Jesus, and if he likewise has seen the wisdom which is mysteriously concealed in the prophets, then he has seen Moses and Elijah in glory, then he has seen them with Jesus."

And a little later:

"After the Word has touched them, the disciples open their eyes and see Jesus only, and no one else. Moses or the Law, and Elijah or Prophecy, they have become one, one with Jesus, who is the Gospel. Thus it is no longer as it was before; no longer do they remain as three, but the three have become one single entity."

In another treatment Origen adds something further to this. The gospel narrative says that Peter wanted to build three tabernacles there, but that he did not know then what he was saying. Indeed, Origen writes, "The Law, the Prophets, and the Gospel do not inhabit three tents, but only one, the only tent; that is, the Church of God."

Not mentioned in this profound observation, with which I really would like to tarry longer, is a figure from the Old Testament who for Origen and his company points to Jesus in a very special way. I refer to Joshua, his namesake; for in the Greek Bible both names are spelled the same way: Iesous. In his preaching on the book of Exodus he comes, in Chapter 17, to the story of Israel's fight against the Amalekites. "Then Moses spoke to Joshua and said, 'Choose men to fight tomorrow against Amalek.'" When Origen comes to this sentence, he says:

"Up to this point the Scripture has never anywhere mentioned the blessed name of Jesus. Here for the first time the brightness of the name shines forth. For the first time Moses makes an appeal to Jesus and says to him, 'Choose men.' Moses calls on Jesus, the Law asks Christ to choose strong men from among the people. Moses cannot choose; it is Jesus alone who can choose strong men, he who has said, 'You did not choose me, but I chose you.' Indeed, he is the head of those who are chosen, the prince of the strong men; it is he who fought against Amalek. He is the one who enters into the house of the strong man, binds him, and makes himself master of the household."

In his collection of sermons on Joshua, probably the last book that he published before his martyrdom, Origen begins with an introduction on the significance of this book of the Bible.

"This significance is not so much to tell us the deeds of Jesus (Joshua) the son of Nun as rather to tell us the mysteries of Jesus my Lord. For it is he who after the death of Moses took over the leadership, he who commanded the camp and who fought against Amalek; and what was indicated there on the mountain, with those outstretched hands, he actualized on the cross, on which in his own person he triumphed over the powers and dominions."

The second sermon deals with a short sentence in the opening part of the book of Joshua: "Moses my servant is dead." The believers must understand well what is being said here, in order to see more clearly how Jesus is ruling now.

"When you see that the temple in Jerusalem lies in ruins, that all this liturgy of the Old Testament has ceased, with all these priestly ranks, these festivals, and these sacrifices, then you see what it means that Moses is dead. A new worship has come in place of the old, which in all its details pointed toward the new."

"When you see that Christ, our paschal lamb, is slain and that we eat the unleavened bread of purity and truth; when you see that the seed in the good earth of the church brings forth fruit thirty, sixty, and a hundredfold — I mean the widows, the virgins, and the martyrs — when you see how the people of Israel are increased in number, the people of those who are born not of blood, nor of the will of man, nor of the will of the flesh, but of God; and when you see the scattered children of God brought together; when you see the people of God celebrate the sabbath, not by refraining from ordinary activities but from works which are sinful; when you see all this, then say, 'God's servant Moses is dead, and Jesus has taken over the leadership.'"

The book of Joshua tells how Israel conquered the Promised Land. For Origen Jesus is the commander of what later would be called "the church militant." As a young man he was a witness when the police arrested his father and took him away for a "trial" with fatal tortures. Only by hiding all his clothes was his mother able to prevent him from running after his father who was being taken away, in order to share his fate with him. When Origen delivers this sermon on Joshua, the emperor Decius is engaged in a well-planned attack on the Christian movement: the idea was systematically and universally to render the leaders of the movement ineffective. They would have to fight, not against Rome's instruments of power, but against cowardice and fear, and the instinct for self-preservation. This is actually an extension of the battle which everyone has to fight who under the leadership of Joshua wants to gain a foothold in the Promised Land. When, in this book of the Bible, God gives the command "not to leave alive anyone that breathed," what does this then signify for us? Here is Origen's answer:

"Suppose that a feeling of anger arises in my heart. Then it can be that I do not go on to commit the deeds themselves, whether because I do not dare, or because I am fearful of the coming judgment. But that is not enough, the Scripture says. You must strive to reach the point that there is no longer any place for even the slightest wave of anger. When the feelings become heated and the mind becomes confused, such agitation is not befitting to a soldier of Jesus, even though it does not result in deeds. This holds true likewise of greed, rancor, or any other vice. As for all these passions, the disciple of Jesus must not let them draw one more breath in his heart. If there remains one bad habit or thought, however small, it will gradually grow and will secretly become strong, and then finally (as the Scripture says) make us return to our vomit; for one whom these things overtake, the last state is worse than the first. The prophetic word in the Psalms is directed to this point: blessed is he who takes your little children and dashes them against the rock. The little children of Babylon are nothing but the wicked thoughts which bring disturbances and confusion to the heart. For this is the significance of the word Babel. One must seize these thoughts while they are still small and in their beginning stages, and then dash them to pieces against the rock which is Christ. At his command one must slay them, in order not to leave anything that breathes within us."

Perhaps a modern reader will find this very moralizing. It would in fact require a great many more and longer citations from Origen in order not to give an altogether false picture of his exposition of the Bible. Unfortunately I must conclude with a couple of supplementary comments.

First, the preacher Origen was also a biblical scholar, in a sense that is more familiar to us. He devoted an enormous amount of time and energy to the comparative study of the biblical texts which were known in his time. The extant fragments of his *Hexapla*, the "sixfold" Bible, are still of inestimable worth. In it, he wrote in six parallel columns the basic text, first in Hebrew letters, then in Greek letters, and then the four Greek translations which were in circulation at that time. Of the Psalms there were even more, so that his work there numbered eight columns. When after many years this giant work was finished, it covered approximately six thousand pages in fifty volumes. Besides this, Origen continued to search diligently for anything that could give him more light on the original meaning of biblical texts. He questioned Jewish rabbis about the real meaning of biblical names, and from his base in Caesarea explored the geography of the biblical inland.

This brings us to a second comment. Regardless of how "spiritual" his exposition was, Origen held fast, as much as possible, to what we call the "historicity" of what is related in the Bible. For him it all had happened just as it was written. But that which happened is, in itself, a signpost pointing to the things which just as really are now happening in Jesus and the church. In this way he defended the reality of revelation and salvation against "Gnostics" who tended to evaporate all this into nothingness. At the same time, by means of his "spiritual" interpretation he was able to maintain the Old Testament against efforts like those of Marcion and his adherents; the latter read the old book "according to the letter" and therefore found it a document that could no longer have any value, now that in Christ the fulness of revelation had come.

In this connection it may be remarked in conclusion that with all his scholarship and originality, Origen intended nothing other than to assimilate and pass on the ancient traditions of the apostolic church. We find most of the "figures" which he points out in the Old Testament already existing earlier, in the New Testament and in the church's writers before him. This is true of Adam and Paradise, Noah and the flood, Abraham and the sacrifice of Isaac, Moses, the exodus through the Red Sea, and many other facts and figures. The instruction in the faith which Origen as a boy had received from his father was already utterly filled with these. It is true that he added to this treasure through his studies and his unwearying reflection upon the biblical texts, all of which appeared to be fresh in his memory.

By way of illustration of this last remark we may note the following. The book of Joshua tells, in the second chapter, about the men who had to spy out the city of Jericho. They found lodging with a harlot, Rahab, who believed that God would give her country and her city to Israel. She got the two spies to promise that she and her family would be spared in the destruction of Jericho and its inhabitants. A red thread from the window of her house on the city wall was to be the sign to Israel's troops that her "house" must be spared.

Now I shall cite a brief passage from Origen. It is seen from this that he knows what the name Rahab signifies in the Hebrew language. The reader who is familiar with the Bible will recognize texts from Isaiah 49 and 54 in which Jerusalem, personified as a woman, both is addressed and is the speaker. Origen says:

"Now let us see who this harlot is. She is called Rahab. This names means 'consecrated.' What consecrated, holy thing can this be other than this church of Christ, brought together from sinners who as it were had been practicing prostitution? She says, 'The place is too narrow for me; make room for me to dwell in' (Isaiah 49:20 RSV). Who has reared these children for me? And she receives the answer, 'Set your stakes out farther and enlarge your tent.'"

Rahab is seen as a "figure" of the church. Origen works this out further and interprets all the details of the narrative in a Christian sense. Of course he does this in his own manner. But as regards contents, he actually does not introduce anything new. What he gives is a bit of ecclesiastical tradition which itself in turn has Jewish roots. For Rahab was a Gentile woman who came to recognize Israel's privileges and was able to join the chosen people, indeed, herself was permitted to become the mother of prophets and kings; one can likewise see in her example how good works are rewarded. Thus Rahab lived on in the esteem of pious Jewish readers of the Bible.

In the New Testament it appears that she, along with the esteem in which she was held, was taken over by the first Christians. Matthew gives her a place in the genealogy of Jesus, perhaps in order to let her, like the Moabite Ruth, show that Jesus is the Messiah for all peoples. Where the epistle to the Hebrews has the great people of faith of the Old Testament pass in review, Rahab also comes on the scene: "By faith Rahab the harlot escaped the fate of those who do not believe, because she had given a friendly welcome to the spies." She is also named by James in connection with faith and works: "Rahab the harlot also was justified for her deeds, because she received the messengers into her house and let them leave by another way."

Before the end of the first century bishop *Clement* of Rome addressed a kind of pastoral writing to the community in Corinth. After having cited the examples of Noah, Abraham, and Lot, he writes: "The harlot Rahab was saved for her faith and hospitality." Then he gives the story in broad outline down to the charge by the spies to bring all her family together in her house at the time of the conquest: "For everyone outside this will be smitten, and will die." Then they charged her, writes Clement, "to prepare a sign; she must let a red cord hang from her house. By this she revealed that through the blood of the Lord there will be redemption for all who believe in God and hope in him. You see, beloved, how there was not only faith, but also a spirit of prophecy in this woman."

The red thread hanging from the window refers to the blood of Christ. Others before Clement probably had noted this reference. The much-traveled seeker *Justin*, who became a Christian around the year 130 after he had tried all the philosophies of his time, brings up this reference in his famous "Dialogue with Trypho the Jew." He does this in connection with the story of the Exodus; therein the Israelites were spared from death and destruction, thanks to the blood of the passover lamb which they had smeared on their doorposts. So will the blood of Christ save those who believe in him, says Justin. The same thing was also indicated by the red thread by which Rahab and her family were saved from destruction. She is the symbol of sinful humanity, who will find deliverance only through faith in the blood of Christ.

Bishop *Irenaeus of Lyons*, martyred in A. D. 202, works out this point in his own way. According to him, Jesus also was thinking of Rahab when he said to the Pharisees, "Tax-collectors and harlots will enter into the kingdom of God ahead of you."

Thus much of what Origen presents to the believers in his sermons reflects a biblical pattern of thinking with which the church had already been familiar for two centuries. It is true that he enriches this tradition with his own emphases which then are further worked out by succeeding generations. Thus he says that no one should have any illusions about that house of Rahab. Anyone who lived outside that house died in the destruction of Jericho, a figure of the world which is perishing. That house of Rahab is the church of Christ: "if anyone abandons that house, then he becomes responsible for his own death."

As a figure of the saving church, the house of Rahab comes to stand alongside other symbols, such as the ark of Noah, to which reference also is already made in the New Testament. And the red thread hanging from the window appears alongside the many other symbols of the passover lamb, and that of other sacrificial rites in the Old Testament. Pieces of wood which appear there can also refer to the wood of the cross. Thus we find in numerous sermons of church fathers the wood of Marah. This was the name of the first well which the Israelites reached after their exodus, when they were very thirsty. But the water was so bitter, *marah*, that they could not drink it. In response to Moses' prayer, God showed him a piece of wood. He threw this into the well, and the water became sweet. This wood is one of the symbols of the cross. This is what makes the water life-giving. The water of the old law, which is undrinkable when it is read according to the letter, also becomes sweet and refreshing when it is touched by the mystery of the cross....

With all this the Old Testament becomes a contemporary, current book: spiritually read, it speaks of the great realities in which the Christian lives and of the fulfillment for which he looks. The biblical scholars in these first centuries were always shepherds of souls, pastors; they preached and gave guidance to the believers. They were "church fathers." They had their believers share in the familiarity with all the ancient figures. Hence the name Rahab only needed to be uttered, and any Christian would think of the red thread and of the blood of Christ and of the house in which one must remain in order to escape eternal perdition. The name Jericho reminded them of a place in Palestine and at the same time of the perishable world which is doomed to destruction because of its unbelief. The children of Babel spoke to them of the evil in their own hearts that ought to be nipped in the bud.

Thus the Old Testament was just as contemporary as the New. In the citations from Origen we saw all sorts of allusions to texts from the epistles of Paul and the others which speak of the mystery of Christ and of the new dimensions of existence into which a person has come through faith. It is somewhat different with the four gospels. They are narrative in character, just as are so many books from the Jewish Bible. They too were spiritually read by the church fathers. The facts all occurred just as they are described there; no one doubts that. But at the same time the narratives are referring to what we now are experiencing and what we anticipate for the future. For the main figure of the gospels lives among us. "He not only healed sicknesses and sufferings when these things happened in the flesh (i. e., in historical reality), but he is still healing them today; he not only came down to men then, but he is still doing this today, and he is present among us." These are Origen's words. But they could also have been written by one of the four evangelists or by a church father in the centuries after Origen. People lived in the belief that Jesus

"not only spoke in the synagogue of the Jews in Galilee, but he is still speaking today, in this meeting among us. We are the Jerusalem over which Jesus still is weeping. We are the dead whom he awakens to life. It is his entire church which is a sinner from the beginning of the world and which now throws herself down before him to anoint his feet and then, purified, to stand up. To the believers of all time, and not to Peter alone, he says, 'If I do not wash you, you will have no part in me. So is it also with his sufferings. Just as in the days of Caiaphas, he is persecuted by false witnesses. From his side there is always the same silence; he does not lift up his voice, but the life of his true disciples speaks for him...."

In the light of all this even the texts of the gospels begin to signify much more than is to be read in them at first glance. I limit myself to two examples from the parables. In these apparently simple stories the incarnate Wisdom has described the mysteries of redemption. In the fifteenth chapter of Luke Jesus tells of a woman who has lost one of her ten pieces of money; she lights her lamp and sweeps her house in order to search for the lost coin.

Pope *Gregory the Great* (590-604) remains entirely in line with the Christian centuries before him, and also with a saying of Jesus himself, when in connection with the word "coin" he thinks of an image. Thus the woman has lost an image, a likeness. Jesus uses this to make us think of man, who was created after God's likeness, but has lost this likeness through his own sin.

The lamp which the woman lights refers to the mystery of the incarnation. Obviously in Gregory's time also little lamps were, just as in the Palestine of Jesus' day, a kind of small pitcher made of baked clay; out of the spout came a wick which continued to burn as long as there was oil in the container. "A lamp is a light in a little pot of earthenware; now light in earthenware is the Deity in the flesh." In Psalm 22 it is suffering, this clay indeed had become hard, and his body dried up like a piece of earthenware." In the fire that was his suffering, this clay indeed had be come hard, and his body acquired new strength in order to rise up again in glory.

When the woman had lighted her lamp, she turned her house inside out. For as soon as the Deity appeared in the flesh, the conscience of men fell into confusion. Therefore the lost coin could be found. For only whenever the conscience is addressed can the likeness to the Creator be restored.

In this vein, Gregory goes on to explain who are meant by the friends and neighbors of the woman, and what it signifies that she had ten coins, of which she lost only one. But to follow this out would require us to relate much more, for example about the nine "choirs" of angels, with whom the Christians of that time were familiar and who in their own way were created in God's image. I prefer to pass on to another example which will say more to the reader.

Jesus' brief story about the good Samaritan quickly began to function among the Christians in the following way. This way of using the passage was already common before Origen and continued through the centuries to be in force. I became acquainted with this interpretation of the Good Samaritan, like the exposition by Gregory just given, from readings in the cloister's choral prayers. What follows here is translated according to a kind of standard exposition which I encountered during my training, in the foreword of a theological manual on the sacraments published in Rome in 1920.

Jesus intended to provide in that story a description of his all-encompassing redemptive work. *A certain man went down from Jerusalem to Jericho.* This man signifies Adam, father and head of all humanity. In him all have sinned. Jerusalem is the paradisiac state of innocence from which this man went down into the changeful condition which is under the dominion of sin, indicated here by Jericho. For the name

of this city means "moon," and the moon with her changeable and sometimes disappearing figure is a symbol of the
wretched and mortal life here on earth, and of all the perishable world.

*He fell into the hands of robbers, who not only took all
that he had, but beat him and then went away, leaving him
half dead.* The robbers represent the devil and his henchmen.
Man fell into their hands when on his own accord he left
behind him the state of innocence. He then was robbed of the
nearness of God which had been given to him. His reason
was no longer capable of ruling over the lower, baser element
within him. So he lay there beside the road, half dead,
robbed of what God had given to him and wounded in the
depths of his nature.

*A priest happened to come down along this way; he saw
him but passed by on the other side. Similarly, a Levite came
along past this place, and he saw him and passed by on the
other side.* These two men signify the priesthood and the
sacrificial ministry of the Old Testament. They could not
help the robbed and wounded man. It is, after all, impossible
for sins to be taken away by means of the blood of bulls and
goats.

*But a Samaritan who was on a journey came in the
vicinity, and when he saw him he was moved with
compassion.* The word "Samaritan" comes from a Hebrew
word that means "someone who watches over or looks after
another." This man is a foreigner. He comes from another
world. He is the one who existed in the form of God and did
not need to regard his equality with God a thing to be
grasped, but who for the sake of us men and of our salvation
came down from heaven, moved by compassion.

*He went to him, bound up his wounds, pouring on oil and
wine, and he set him on his own donkey, brought him to an
inn, and cared for him.* The donkey signifies the body in
which he came to us, and on it he placed the wounded man;

did he not bear our sins in his own body on the cross? The bandages with which he bound up the wounds after he had poured oil and wine on them signify the medicines of the sacraments. And the inn is the church which he himself founded on earth in order therein to provide refreshment for travelers on the way to eternity.

The next day he gave the innkeeper two pieces of money and said, 'Take care of him, and if you have more expenses, I will repay you when I come again.' The next day is the time after his resurrection and before his ascension to the Father. The innkeeper represents the leaders of the church. The two coins which he gave to the innkeeper are the gospel and the sacraments of the new law. He pointed to these when at his departure he charged his disciples to teach and to baptize all nations. And they were to do this "until I return," for this Jesus will return from heaven just as he was taken up into heaven.

8. In the hand of religious leaders, states, and churches

One could call the biblical thinking of the church fathers "symbolic." It is well characterized by what Huizinga wrote about the symbolic thinking of the Middle Ages. With reference to the "things" in the following text, including the walnut, one must think of the biblical words and the realities which they signify.

"Symbolist thought permits of an infinity of relations between things. Each thing may denote a number of distinct ideas by its different special qualities, and a quality may also have several symbolic meanings. The highest conceptions have symbols by the thousand. Nothing is too humble to represent and to glorify the sublime. The walnut signifies Christ; the sweet kernel is His divine nature, the green and pulpy outer peel is His humanity, the wooden shell between is the cross. Thus all things raise the thoughts to the eternal; being thought of as symbols of the highest, in a constant gradation, they are all transfused by the glory of divine majesty."

In the reflection on the Bible in the line of the church fathers there resonates in every text what Huizinga calls "a harmonic accord of symbols." Thereby every biblical word acquires "an additional value," and together with all others points to the central mystery of Christ and his church.

Perhaps this holds true for the book of Psalms more than for many another part of the Bible. Bishop Augustine (died A. D. 430) regularly preached expository sermons on the Psalms. Around the year 417 he published a number of these. This book, *Enarrationes in Psalmos,* is one of his most extensive works, twice as long as his famous book on *The City of God.* Careful investigation has shown that 119 of these sermons were given extemporaneously and copied down by a stenographer, and further that he dictated 86 expositions at home in order to make the volume more complete. In the expositions which were taken down by stenographers, Augustine sometimes confesses that he has made preparations on a psalm other than the one which has just been read by the lector. Then he improvises. Anyone who is somewhat familiar with his style and is no longer frightened off by certain forms of that style which are peculiar to the times can only marvel at the sureness with which he sees in every verse a reference to Christ. When he sees this name he thinks at one and the same time of a person and of a worldwide fellowship. Thus it is said in the title of Psalm 61 that it is a prayer of David. For Augustine it is the son of David, Christ, who is praying here, the head and the members, all believers throughout the whole earth.

"In the speaker in this psalm we must recognize ourselves and no one else. By ourselves I do not mean only those who are present here, but all of us over the whole world from east to west. And to show that it really is the voice of all of us, he speaks as though it were one single man. But it is not one single man, but in this one man our unity is speaking. For through Christ we all are one man. The head of this one man is in heaven, but the members toil here on earth. Note what he says with reference to this toiling existence."

This already appears where the psalmist (in the Latin translation which Augustine used) says that he cries to God "from the ends of the earth." This cannot be an individual. It can only be the whole church that is here addressing herself to God, and that out of her afflictions. For all members of Christ must experience the course of his life, and thus even his afflictions. Just as he overcame, so will the Christians, following after him, rise above their afflictions. Just after this the Latin text of the psalm says, "You set me high upon the rock."

"Therefore it is no wonder that in the midst of the afflictions he cries from the ends of the earth. And why is he not overcome? High on the rock you set me. Indeed, now we understand who it is that is crying from the ends of the earth. Think of the gospel: On this rock I will build my church. Thus it is she whom he willed to build upon the rock that is crying over all the earth. But who then has become this rock, to be able to build the church thereupon? Listen to Paul: Now the rock was Christ. Thus it is on him that we are built. Therefore this rock on which we are built was earlier buffeted by wind, flood, and rain, when Christ was tested by the devil. So this is the foundation on which he willed to establish you. Our cry therefore is not a fruitless outcry, but it is heeded. Great is the confidence on which we rest. High on the rock you set me."

I shall resist the temptation to cite still more from this "exposition" in which Augustine a few times comes to sublime expression of what constitutes the kernel of the Christian experience. And this holds true of innumerable passages in this priceless book of *Enarrationes*. For what I am concerned with is the role of the Psalms in the prayers of the church, and particularly of those whose vocation is prayer, namely the monks. The stately singing of the Psalms at many hours of the day and of the night determined the atmosphere in which innumerable ones of them came to the loftiest forms of contemplation.

So it went through the centuries. When the Spaniard *Dominic* in the beginning of the thirteenth century breaks through the monastic forms and founds religious communities as operational bases for preaching to the people, he holds fast to the reflective recitation of the Psalms. He asked his colleagues to know the epistles of Paul by heart, as good representatives of "the Apostle" in this modern time with its profound alterations in the structures of society. He says nothing about the book of Psalms. It is taken for granted that they already know it by heart. On their months-long trips on foot, crisscrossing the Europe of those days, he and his companions recited the Psalms, the prayers of the Christ in whose continuing activity they knew their own lifework to be incorporated.

Thomas Aquinas, a disciple of Dominic, indicates, in the foreword of his "exposition of David's Psalms," written about 1253, in his own way why the book of Psalms plays such an important role in the life of the church. Thomas' method is systematic. The "matter" of this book, according to him, coincides with the whole of theology. All of the four great themes of theology are treated in it: creation, salvation history, restoration through the incarnation, and the final consummation. On the third point he remarks, "All that concerns that restoration through the incarnation is treated so clearly in this book of the Bible that it almost resembles a gospel rather than prophecy." This treatment of all the themes of theology also is the reason why "the psalter is the most extensively used book in the church; it actually contains the entire Scripture." And a little later, "The matter of this book is Christ and his people."

As for the literary form, one finds in the Bible the narrative form in the historical books; the hortatory, admonitory, and commanding form, which is used in the laws, the prophetic books, and the didactic books; and the form of discussion, especially in Job and in Paul. But there is also the form of prayer and praise; this is used in the psalter: "All that is expressed in the other biblical books in the above-mentioned forms is found here in the style of praise and prayer."

The theology of Thomas was, for all its conceptual character, deeply rooted in biblical soil. With his successors we see the tree more and more cut off from these roots. There remains a barren play with concepts, branches without leaves and blooms in which, to put it in the style of the church fathers, birds can no longer build a nest. Only in a couple of meditative cloisters is Bible reading after the fashion of Origen and Augustine still a well from which people draw living water.

In 1501 Erasmus made an attempt to render this well once again accessible to the ordinary believer. At that time he wrote his "Handbook for the Christian soldier," which was printed in 1503 and especially after 1510 was widely distributed and much read, before long even in various vernacular tongues. According to him Christians must learn to read the Scripture as did Augustine, Ambrose, and Jerome, and especially Origen, who occupies first place among the interpreters of the Bible. The believing reader must search for the deeper significance behind the literal meaning of the biblical texts. "The Spirit" intends to reach him through "the flesh" of the letter and to affect him in the only thing that it all really concerns, and that is the mystery of Christ. Of course this holds true for the Old Testament. What is the point of reading the stories of the forming of Adam out of clay and of Eve out of the rib, and all these other things, if one does not seek something more behind them? "What kind of difference is there between the reading of the Old Testament books such as Kings and Judges and those of the historical works of Livy, if one does not pay attention to the allegorical significance? Everywhere, and especially in the Old Testament, one must minimize the flesh of the Scripture and work out the spiritual, mystical sense."

This is true also of the gospels. There too there is flesh and spirit. It is Christ himself who says that the flesh profits nothing, and that only the spirit makes alive. "I surely would not have dared to say this in such strong terms. It would have been sufficient to say that the flesh does indeed have some value but the spirit has much more. Now the Truth himself says it so strongly: 'The flesh profiteth nothing.'" Erasmus somewhere cites a whole series of biblical texts which speak of spring water that brings refreshment and healing for men. In these we may see indicated the mysteries of the Scripture. "What does the water that is hidden deep in the earth signify, other than the mystery that is enclosed within the letter?"

Historians disagree over the influence of Erasmus on the Reformation. It appears to me that the manner of reading the Bible which he advocates will yet be practiced sometime in pious circles. But it presupposes a developed capacity for symbolic thinking. The intellectual atmosphere of the succeeding centuries was not conducive to this capacity. And in our time it is not just any- and everybody who will forthwith declare that the "symbolic" reading of the Bible is no longer possible for modern man.

So much for the first of the three methods of interpretation which I have proposed to sketch in this section. In the fourth century still another use of the Bible came into vogue alongside this one. I refer to the more or less literal application of the Old Testament. With the emperor Constantine, who died in 336, Christianity became the state religion. After the fall of the Roman Empire then we see the beginning of what was quickly to become "Christendom." This term carries with it the idea that the whole life of society is based on Christian principles. The populace of the new Europe is "the people of God." There happened there on the large scale what the Old Testament shows with respect to the people of Israel. They were destined, as a nation, to actualize in their national structures the demands of the covenant, in particular the exclusive worship of the true God. These structures were to protect the nation against influences from the heathen nations surrounding them.

Very early, shortly after Constantine's time, zealots for the Christian religion appealed to Deuteronomy 13, with its harsh rules against anyone who worships another deity, or who attempts to prompt members of the nation to practice such idolatry. These measures now were regarded as binding upon the Christian emperors.

One of the great advocates of the Oecumene, the Dominican Yves Congar, recently gave a large number of examples of the influence which the literal application of the Old Testament had on the life of society in various areas of early Christendom. He cites the development of a body of religious leaders distinguished by rank, whose primary function is to conduct liturgical services, and for whom rites of consecration were worked out in line with the prescriptions of Moses. Another example is the assessment of tithes for the support of these religious leaders. In the eighth century kings were anointed according to the example of Saul and David. Then people began also to consecrate churches with a ceremony following the laws of Exodus and Leviticus, with sprinkling, anointing, and incense. In Christian Ireland in the seventh century the observance of Sunday was rejected in favor of that of the sabbath.

One of the court theologians of Charlemagne (768-814) was named Alcuin. Students of his writings on politics and in the social area have demonstrated that four-fifths of the terms which he used came from the Old Testament. For him Charlemagne is the new king Josiah, called to restore the worship of the true God in all its purity. But Alcuin usually calls him the chosen David. The conclusion of Deuteronomy 17 was held up as a mirror before Charlemagne and many Christian rulers after him. Therefore, however, the wars which they fought also were considered wars of God's people. Whenever people with pacifist tendencies appealed to the new spirit which Christ has brought, the theologians would refer them to Jesus, who spoke so approvingly of the officer in Capernaum, and to Cornelius in Acts 10, also a military leader, and to the fact that John the Baptist did indeed give all sorts of admonitions to the soldiers who came to him, but did not denounce their profession.

Congar has also published a study of the vicissitudes of a saying which God addressed to Jeremiah when he called him to function as a prophet: "Behold, I have set you over nations and kingdoms, to pluck up and to break down, to build and to plant." He shows that in the early centuries bishops and priests saw their own pastoral task expressed in this text, often in combination with words of Jesus to Peter. Such a man as Pope Gregory the Great had, according to a biographer in the eighth century, put them into practice, because he indeed had "everywhere pulled up the roots of evil and destroyed them, and planted and built up virtues." Later the saying began to function to the benefit of the popes, to whom God was supposed to have given the fullness of spiritual and temporal power.

A similar use of the Bible is to be seen in the famous text about the two swords. A study of this subject begins with a difficulty which Charlemagne presented to his theologian Alcuin. According to the evangelist Luke, Jesus commanded his disciples, just before his arrest, to sell their cloaks and to buy a sword. When they answered that they had two swords, he said, "That is enough." Peter must have used one of these two swords to cut off the ear of Malchus. But then Jesus says, "Put your sword in the sheath, for anyone who uses the sword shall die by the sword." Now how can this be? asks Charlemagne. "If the sword is the word of God, and if the Lord, in his command to buy a sword, meant that word of God, how then can one say that all who receive the word of God shall perish through that word of God?" Charlemagne had stumbled over a contradiction in the gospels and he did

not find his way out of it with the help of a symbolic meaning. He did not know that the question had already been
treated by many interpreters of the Scripture in the centuries
before him, and just as little did he suspect that in the
centuries after him this text about the two swords would
come to serve as a weapon in passionate disputes between
popes and emperors over the supreme power.

Biblical texts also played a major role in summoning
Christianity to the Crusades, and in the moral justification of
them. Over against the *jihad*, the "holy war" of Islam which
posed a fatal threat to Christendom, the latter placed her
own holy war against the heretics and unbelievers. One of
the aims was the conquest of the holy land. The book of
Joshua provides specific guidelines for the campaign, even to
the details such as the accompanying of the armies of the
crusaders by priests. The stories of the Maccabeans' fight
against the armies of the heathen also served as models. The
Jerusalem of the prophecies and the Psalms, since Paul's
epistle to the Galatians located "above," now once again
becomes the earthly city, to which the crusaders would bring
deliverance and glory. It is they who begin to bring to
fulfillment Isaiah 60 and such texts as Zechariah 12.
Jerusalem would be trodden by the Gentiles, Jesus had said,
"until the times of the Gentiles should be fulfilled." The
crusaders now are bringing this fulfillment, they who
according to Jesus' word have denied themselves and have
taken the cross upon themselves.

Nowadays people like to bring the history of the crusaders
forward to relate it to the western invasion of which Palestine
in our time has become the suffering victim. But there is a
later undertaking of Christendom which offers a better
parallel, with respect to the method of colonization as well as
to the biblical justification of it. I refer to the Spanish
conquest of America.

In the year 1513 the Spanish king Ferdinand appointed a
commission of theologians. In the new world some Domini-

cans had taken up for the rights of the natives. At that moment a valuable fleet lay ready to depart on a new expedition. But King Ferdinand would not let it sail until the theologians had found a moral basis for their war against the Indians. The commission allowed itself to be convinced by the biblical argumentation of Enciso.

He defended the thesis that God had entrusted the Indies to Spain, just as he had given the promised land to the Jews:

"Moses sent Joshua to the inhabitants of Jericho, the first city in the promised land of Canaan, to demand that they abandon their city because it belonged to the people of Israel, in view of the fact that God had given it to them. And when the people of Jericho did not give up their city, Joshua besieged them and killed them all, except for a woman who had protected his spies. And after this Joshua conquered the entire land of Canaan by armed force; many were killed, and the prisoners of war were made slaves and served the people of Israel. And all this was done by the will of God, because they were idolators."

This last point was very clever of Enciso. He knew the aversion of the Spaniards to any form of idolatry. Evidently no one doubted his interpretation of Israel's ancient history. He completed his plea by explaining that the pope, who was God's representative, had given the Indies to Spain, and along with them the idolatrous inhabitants of these lands, with the aim that the Catholic king should introduce Christianity there. Therefore, he said, "it is perfectly justifiable that the king should send men to demand of these idolatrous Indians that they yield their land to him; for it is given to him by the pope. If the Indians are not willing to do this, he may justly wage war against them, kill them, and make slaves of the prisoners of war, just as Joshua treated the inhabitants of the land of Canaan."

Bartolomeo de las Casas, who was drawn to the new world as a colonist in 1502, began after 1514 to devote himself entirely to the battle for the human rights of the Indians.

Contrary to the public opinion of the Spanish world empire, he continued to maintain that the Indians are men in the full sense of the word; he even defended the view that must have sounded like an enormity, that the Indians in certain respects were more civilized than the Spaniards who had invaded their land with violence. He published important books on the culture and the history of the peoples of central America. Thus he described the ancient temples in Mexico, which according to him equalled the pyramids of Egypt, a fact that archaeologists in our century have rediscovered and that now is confirmed by numerous tourists. A high point in the life of this great defender of the defenseless was his public dispute with Sepulveda that took place in Valladolid in 1551.

Sepulveda found a biblical argument in Jesus' parable of the wedding feast. In it the Lord says, "Compel them to come in." Therefore the Spaniards might use force against the natives. Las Casas had to be very cautious in answering this argument. For emperors and popes also had used it, and the inquisition was lying in wait. He explained that in this text no external compulsion was meant, but "an internal compulsion by the inspiration of God and by the ministry of his angels." For this interpretation he could appeal to one of the great church fathers.

Alongside the "figurative" interpretation and the literal application in practice, a third form of use of the Bible may only be cited: people adduce texts in order to prove their own dogmatic correctness. This use comes strongly to the fore after the disintegration of Christendom. During the Counter-Reformation the church of Rome locked herself up entirely within her own bulwarks. Protestant churches arose around Luther, Calvin, Zwingli, and others. Very soon the movements solidified in more or less well-knit structured church communities, and their doctrine solidified in confessional writings. Thus it arose from this state of things that one and the same biblical text could evoke directly opposing reactions. If a Catholic hears Jesus saying to Peter, "Upon this rock I will build my church," he thinks of the pope and of St. Peter in Rome. A Protestant upon hearing these words realizes that in any case it cannot be the papacy that is meant.

When in the eighteenth century the "age of reason" dawns, the churches begin to have difficulty with their old doctrinal positions concerning holy Scripture and the faith. A friend recently showed me a book that the Groningen professor P. van Limburg Brouwer published in 1847. He taught the classics, but felt himself heavily affected by what was going on in his days in the Protestant churches in the Netherlands. That was a struggle between a group who wanted to bring the Christian faith into harmony with reason and feeling, and in this connection wanted to place the inspiring person of Christ in the center of the life of faith, and other groups who wanted to hold more or less strictly to the old formulations. In the book referred to, *Het leesgezelschap van Diepenbeek*, van Limburg Brouwer describes the effects of these ecclesiastical controversies in a small village community. It is a kind of satire, obviously written with pleasure and with a touch of malicious satisfaction. I have read it with pleasure. But in a reader of the temperament of the author of Ecclesiastes, or in one who is somewhat pessimistic by nature, it can raise the question: were not the conflicts then exactly like they are now? is there really anything new under the sun? It seems to me that since 1840 developments have occurred which have caused the opposing positions now to be differently situated.

2

The Historical Approach

"What we have always thought about that bit of the past must be wrong! It is a historical impossibility!" Thus one may perhaps state the surprise which struck a number of historians in Europe around 1800. They felt themselves suddenly driven by the passion to use every possible means to search out "the facts as they really were." A typical representative of them is sometimes seen in Georg Niebuhr, the German statesman who in 1810 began with the publication of his history of Rome. Up until then the earliest history of Rome had been repeated from generation to generation just as it was written by Titus Livius, who issued his detailed historical works about the beginning of the Christian era. This was the story of the founding of Rome in 753 B. C. by Romulus and Remus, of the first seven kings, and so on. Niebuhr showed that the narrative given by Livy was to a large extent built upon legends, and he even pointed out what he called "mythical" elements therein.

Thus in his book a bit of ancient history was critically examined. Niebuhr posed such questions as: "Where did my source get his data? What is the historical value of this source? What was Livy's aim in writing? What were his assumptions and his prejudices?"

This need to search out something as far back as possible had already long ago become customary in other areas of scholarship, particularly in the natural sciences. But the terrain of history had hardly been entered with this intention. Hence the vigorous investigation by Niebuhr gave a powerful impetus to the development of what is called "critical historical study."

Should this investigation come to a halt at the boundaries of the sacred terrain of the Bible? After all, this book too is a document from antiquity. It contains numerous stories from earlier times, just as does the work of Livy. May questions like those of Niebuhr also be posed to the Bible? May one also in relation to this book institute an investigation into the origin of stories and the historical reliability of the writers?

Many Christians stood up for their conviction that this may not be done. It is permissible to use the help of scientific scholarly means to trace the original wording of the biblical text (textual criticism), and as fully as possible to grasp the meaning of it (with the study of the Semitic languages and of Greek). Ever since the sixteenth century this had been done on an ever increasing scale. No objection can be raised against these studies from the perspective of the faith. But for a believing Christian, at least, there can be no thought of "historical criticism" in relation to the Bible, such as Niebuhr had applied to Livy. This after all is implied in the fact that the Bible is given by God, "inspired" down to the last detail. Therefore the Bible is free of any error. God cannot lie or deceive. Now what is called "historical criticism" starts out from the assumption that there is something on this point to investigate. It assumes that the actual course of events could have been other than the biblical narratives give us to understand. Thus there could be something untrue in the Bible. By taking this as a starting point, this investigation undermines the divine authority of the Bible, and therewith the entire belief that is based upon this Bible.

This was the conviction of a great many Christians in the church. Hence it was that the protests increased in number and intensity when biblical scholars began to employ the new instrument of "historical criticism" in their research. Prof. J. Lutz, a clergyman who from 1834 to his death in 1844 held a professorship of Bible in Basel, was concerned over "the steadily widening gulf between the ecclesiastical belief of the people and the biblical interpretation of the scholars." Forty years later we see one of the greatest biblical scholars of that time, *Julius Wellhausen*, request a transfer from the theological faculty to the philosophical faculty. In a letter of April 5, 1882, he reminded the Prussian Minister of Culture that his request of two years earlier still had not been approved. In this letter he wrote: "I became a theologian because I was interested in the scientific treatment of the Bible. It has only gradually become evident to me that a professor in theology also has the practical task of preparing the students for service in the Evangelical Church, and that in this practical task I fall short, indeed, that in spite of all reserve on my part, I am rather making my hearers unfit for their office."

This last remark is noteworthy. We have seen that the "sanctification" of the Torah, and therewith the idea of "divine inspiration," was connected with the organization of the Jews into a clearly marked-off community. Could the resistance of the official churches to historical investigation which appeared to deny this inspiration be connected with their own concern to stand apart as a community, as "true church"? Perhaps we shall be able to say more about this after we have seen, by means of a couple of examples, how profoundly the new approach affected the train of thought with which the Christians had been familiar since the origin of the church.

1. Moses and the Pentateuch

All through the centuries it had been thought that the first five books of the Bible were written by Moses, under inspiration from God. It was one large work, already before Christ's time divided into five (pente) scrolls (teuchos), and therefore called "Pentateuch." Apart from a solitary critical spirit here and there, before the nineteenth century no one had doubted this idea. There was not even any reason to do so. The second of the five books, Exodus, begins with the story of Moses' birth. He remains the major figure in the story, even in the following books, down to the conclusion of the fifth, Deuteronomy, in which his death is described. Moses writes that he is a descendant of Levi, one of the twelve sons of the patriarch Jacob, who himself was a grandson of Abraham. The latter's forefathers were known by name back to and including the first, Adam. What Moses wrote in the first book, Genesis, about events which had happened long before his birth, he therefore could have known from oral tradition. Besides, he himself tells how intimately he communed with God, as friend with friend. He could, so to speak, know from firsthand account how the creation of the world had taken place.

Moreover, Moses tells more than once that he had put down in writing the facts which he had experienced and witnessed, and furthermore that he recorded in a book the laws which God had dictated to him. Alongside these statements of Moses himself, in other books of the Old Testament several times reference is made to the lawbook which he had given, "the Law of Moses." Weightiest of all, however, was the solemn declaration of Christ, who said to the Jews: "If you had believed Moses, then you would also believe me, because he wrote concerning me. If you do not believe what he wrote, how could you then believe what I am saying?"

Hence the shock which went through the churches when biblical scholars declared, "This cannot be; Moses cannot have written the first five books of the Bible; this is a historical impossibility."

Anyone who was able to listen to their arguments calmly was quickly convinced, particularly if he was familiar with insights which had already earlier broken through. In 1753 the physician of the French royal court, who had enough free time to practice other sciences also, published a book with the clear title, "Conjectures about the documents which Moses appears to have used in the writing of the book of Genesis." He had already seen that various "hands" could be demonstrated in the book of Genesis. "Now that is simply historically impossible," said the biblical scholars a century later. Such an enormous work as the Pentateuch cannot have been written about 1400 B. C., and certainly not with the aid of already existing "documents." For most of the stories and collections of laws which form the Pentateuch can only have arisen in a highly developed society. It is inconceivable that the "founder" of Israel could have produced such a work straight out of his own resources, in a social and cultural void, in the desert in which he is said to have spent the last forty years of his life, which were also the first years of Israel's existence as a nation. Moreover, the Pentateuch did not yet exist in its present form during the reigns of David, Solomon, and the succeeding kings, during the time of the great prophets and the Babylonian exile. For not only is there nothing said about the Pentateuch in reliable biblical accounts of these centuries, but besides, much of the history is utterly incomprehensible if we assume that the Pentateuch did exist. But if one sees the "documents" out of which the work is assembled as having developed in the course of this history, then one also gains a clear insight into the development of Israel's religion and the emergence of the Pentateuch.

This clear insight was provided primarily by the brilliant German biblical scholar whom we have already mentioned, Julius Wellhausen. Beginning in 1870 he wrote books and articles which set forth his theory about the development of the Pentateuch which amounted to the following. The *foundation* was laid shortly after Solomon, about *850 B. C.*, by an author in the kingdom of Judah whose name is unknown to us. He wrote a history which began with the creation of Adam and Eve in Paradise and the fall, Cain's murder of his brother, the flood, and the tower of Babel. This was followed by stories about Abraham, Isaac, and Jacob, the sojourn of Jacob's sons in Egypt, the exodus under the leadership of Moses, the divine manifestation on Sinai, some laws, and the journey through the wilderness down to the death of Moses. *About 750*, a century later, someone in the northern kingdom of Israel wrote *a similar history*, which he began with the life of Abraham. After the fall of the northern kingdom these two narrative works were *combined* into one, *around the year 650*. The book of the law which was "discovered" in the temple in Jerusalem during the reign of king Josiah in the year 621 corresponds to the book of *Deuteronomy*, the last part of Moses' work. In the middle of the next century, *around 550 B. C.*, it was combined with the large historical work. During and after the exile the priests worked out a large number of liturgical prescriptions, and on the basis of liturgical calendars they designed a system of chronology for Israel's past and for that of mankind from the creation. *About the year 400* these elements were united with the combined historical work and Deuteronomy into the complex whole which we designate as "the books of Moses" or the Pentateuch.

Utterly shocking! thus the Law of Moses had come into being a thousand years later than people had believed all through the centuries, not written by the greatest inspired person of the Old Testament, but by unknown people from a much later time! Wellhausen contended that these writers, so many centuries after Moses, could not have had much reliable information about his person and work. Thus one must attribute to the imagination of later generations the clear picture of Moses that the Pentateuch gives. According to Wellhausen, nothing at all can be said with certainty about the patriarchs of Israel; one can only know how these writers of 850 and 750 B. C. conceived of their distant ancestors of a thousand years earlier. Thus Wellhausen and all these other modernists flatly denied the church's dogma of inspiration, not only by denying that Moses had anything to do with the writing of the Pentateuch, but also by plainly assuming that this book was full of untruths. Still more, according to them Christ had lied when he said that Moses had written about him. This was nothing less than blasphemy!

Indeed, the whole theory was a product of utter unbelief. Those who held the theory constantly talked about "historical impossibilities," about "making the historical course of things transparent," and so on. As though such overwhelming deeds of God like the exodus and the revelation at Sinai and the inspiration of Moses might be measured by our sinful human standards! As though any attitude would be fitting here other than one of reverence and gratitude, which would silence all questions of human curiosity!

Wellhausen was regarded by believers in the church as "antichrist." He suffered severely under attacks from this quarter, some of which were worse than unchristian. As fierce as was the indignation, just so intense was the fear that this new approach would undermine the entire system of Christian dogmas. Hence it was also that the new theory set off an avalanche of articles, books, and pamphlets, in which all the arguments were refuted with lesser or greater expertness.

The church of Rome, characterized by her teaching authority, very soon reacted with an unequivocal rejection of the theory. A couple of her biblical scholars had said that they could agree with the new view of the Pentateuch. They thought that this view did not need to come into conflict with the doctrine of the divine inspiration of the Bible, so long as one understood this doctrine correctly. In the Netherlands this opinion was defended by the Limburg priest Henri Poels, a man as intelligent as he was energetic. During his studies at Louvain he had become acquainted with the new historical method. He defended it in a long article on "De oorsprong van de Pentateuch" ("The origin of the Pentateuch"), published in *De Katholiek* in December 1898. It was intended to be the first of a series, but the promised sequel never appeared. As early as the beginning of 1899 the bishop of Haarlem presented "the Poels case" to Rome. As a result this biblical scholar was unable to assume the professorship in the priests' seminary at Roermond which had been intended for him, and he was appointed chaplain at Venlo.

The resistance of the Roman theologians was understandable. They saw in the new view of the Pentateuch one of the expressions of "Modernism." This was the name they gave to the thinking then current which was dominated by the insight into the historical — and thus changeable — evolutionary nature of everything, even of religion. This insight seemed to be irreconcilable with the Catholic faith as the latter had taken shape in the church of Rome. The church regarded herself as the protectress of the revealed truth, which had been entrusted to her by God and was fixed in unchangeable formulations which were valid for all time, "dogmas." Concepts such as historical development and change appeared to be just as much in conflict with this position as did the introduction into these matters of truth of personal experience and feeling, to which the Modernists assigned so much value.

The papal Biblical Commission, established in 1902 to give guidance to biblical study and interpretation in the church, began in 1905 to issue a kind of rules for teaching, in the form of answers to doubts that were presented to them. They formulated these doubts (dubia) so carefully that they always could be answered with a simple yes or no, which left nothing to be desired in terms of clarity.

Already in June 1906 the question of the Pentateuch arose. The meaning of the yes-and-no answers to the four questions amounted to the following: "The arguments of present-day historical criticism are not strong enough in the face of the centuries-old tradition which regards Moses as the writer of the Pentateuch; it is possible that he made use of oral and written sources and that he entrusted to secretaries the actual work of putting it in writing; slight variations, additions, and (of course inspired) glosses also might have slipped into the text during the centuries of their being handed down; but the substance of the work goes back to Moses himself."

Objections very soon arose from Catholic biblical scholars. They could understand that the ecclesiastical authority wanted to keep the mass of the faithful free from any sudden encounter with the new view which would only unnecessarily confuse them. But surely the pope did not intend to put an end to the scientific and thus open approach to the matter by serious investigators?

"That is precisely what I intend," answered Pius X in a declaration of November 18, 1907: every Catholic must in conscience submit to the already issued and yet-to-be-issued pronouncements of the Biblical Commission; he incurred grave guilt before God if he attacked them in any way whatever in word or in writing.

Therewith an end was made of all research in Catholic circles. Anyone who published anything that exhibited traces of the new theory about the Pentateuch was immediately called to order, sometimes removed from his office, a step coupled with dramatic and sometimes painful developments.

The consequences were felt in the training of priests throughout the world. If the students did hear anything about the Pentateuch, it was almost exclusively the proofs of the authorship of Moses, and the detailed refutation of the arguments which the "rationalists" and "unbelieving criticism" had brought forward. When Catholic young men began their study for the priesthood with some interest in the holy Scripture, they quickly lost it as a result of this apologetic approach, which was characteristic also of the treatment of other parts of the Bible.

It was only in 1943 that the embargo was lifted. The upheavals of war did not prevent Roman circles from celebrating a jubilee: fifty years earlier Pope Leo XIII had given directions, in his encyclical *Providentissimus Deus*, for modern interpretation of the Bible. A half century later Pius XII was ruling; he had placed his confidence in Father Bea, a Jesuit and a great authority on modern biblical scholarship. The latter made use of his position to get the pope to write, with reference to that jubilee, a new encyclical, with the opening words *Divino afflante Spiritu* ("Through the divine inspiring Spirit..."). This letter contained an urgent recommendation to Catholic biblical scholars to employ, in determining the meaning of the sacred texts, all the modern critical methods, as well as the increasing amount of information which was being offered by excavations and deciphered texts from the ancient Near East. The letter explicitly provided protection for the Catholic researchers against attacks from the side of orthodoxy: "All other children of the church must remember that they must judge the efforts of these stalwart laborers in the vineyard of the Lord (the biblical scholars!) not only with justice and fairness, but also with the greatest love. They must avoid the unhealthy tendency to think that everything that is new must for that reason be contested or be regarded with suspicion."

A little later he speaks further about the liberty of the Catholic interpreters, "this true freedom of the children of God which both faithfully adheres to the Church's teaching and gratefully accepts and uses, as a gift of God, all that profane sciences have provided."

After the war the salutary effects of Pius' encyclical of 1943 appeared in all sorts of books and articles. The Catholic interpreters of the Bible felt themselves relieved of the heavy pressure which had prevented them from making their insights fruitful for others. Instead of a cramped apologetic for Moses' authorship, in which they themselves had long since ceased to believe, seminary professors now could devote their time to the treatment of the actual message of the Pentateuch. It is self-explanatory that at first this was successful only with a few; they were not at all trained for this kind of biblical interpretation.

In the sentence just quoted about the freedom of the children of God there was also something about the faithful adherence to the church's teaching. The historical approach now was allowed for the Bible. Was it not an obvious thing now also to apply it to later, non-biblical formulations of the faith? Had not the dogmas and the thought-out system of truths of the faith that was built upon these dogmas also actually developed historically, and were they not therefore subject to alteration? In 1951 Pius XII wrote his encyclical *Humani Generis*, which on certain points appeared once again to limit the freedom of investigation which had been granted in 1943. But *Divino afflante* had done its work and it remained an important factor in the stormy developments which led to the second Vatican Council.

This was due primarily to Pope John, who brought into the Vatican from his farm background a robust common sense and from his later career a strong historical concern. But his initiative fell into well prepared soil. There had to be an ecumenical council. It surely was not by accident that it was Father Bea, the man behind the encyclical of 1943, now a cardinal, who was given the task of drawing together the ecumenical endeavors.

As for the world of the Protestant churches, the battle over Moses and the Pentateuch there was no less intense. But it naturally was waged locally, and the teaching authority that defended the tradition was not embodied in an individual, such as the Roman pope, but in "bodies" such as the denominational council, classis, or synod. There too preachers and theologians were called to order, and sometimes were relieved of their posts, with the dramatic developments that go with such events.

The more a Protestant church fellowship was oriented to the past in its thinking about the faith, the later was the change in coming. In 1952 Professor G. Aalders of the Free University in Amsterdam published an introduction to the books of the Old Testament, under the title of *Oud-Testamentische Kanoniek* ("The canon of the Old Testament"). In a very elaborate chapter on "de Wet" ("the Law") he comes to the conclusion that the major part of the Pentateuch must have been written by Moses himself or at least under his direction, in the course of which documents from an earlier time also probably were used. There are only a couple of pieces in the work which were added to the book after the death of Moses. In the time of the judges the Pentateuch must have been known among the Israelites "practically in its present form." The final editing of the work must have taken place under "the reign of Saul, or at the latest in the first years of David's reign in Hebron." Thus Aalders can maintain all the other data of the Bible in their most literal sense, even the solemn declaration of Christ already mentioned above. According to him, it is better to give the ordinary meaning of "letters" to the word *grammasin* in the Greek text; here the Savior is setting his own spoken word over against the written words of Moses. "If you do not believe what he wrote...." Then Moses needs only to have written the major part of the Pentateuch and not the entire work.

It is a testimony to the rapidity of developments that this view now belongs to the past, even among the theologians of the Gereformeerde Kerken.

It would, after all, compel them, in the study of modern commentaries and handbooks in the area of the Old Testament, and of works on the historical developments in ancient Israel, to note their objections on almost every page.

2. Isaiah and his book

The gospels, the book of Acts, and the epistles contain more references to Isaiah than to any other book of the Old Testament; hence the veneration of Isaiah as the greatest of the prophets. God permitted him to catch a glimpse, more clearly than the others, of the great work which God was going to perform at the end of time. Isaiah saw the Immanuel, born of a maiden, the child who at his birth awakens joy because the universal government is placed upon his shoulders.... He also saw the man who, endowed with the sevenfold gift of the Spirit, as servant or slave of the Lord takes upon himself the proclamation of God's will, becomes a victim of the sinfulness of men, and is offered up by God as a sin-offering for many.... Isaiah further spoke of the glory of the heavenly Jerusalem, of the destruction of death at the end of time, and of so many other realities with which the Christian is familiar.

Hence the shock which the German scholar *Bernard Duhm* set in motion in 1893 with his commentary on the book of Isaiah. According to him it is only in the first part of the book that we have some utterances of the great Isaiah (approximately 740 B. C.). Chapters 40-55 are from the pen of an unknown writer who worked about one and a half centuries later, during the exile in Babylon. This latter author knew something of the first successes of King Cyrus; thus he wrote in the time after 550 B. C. What the book of Isaiah offers in the last eleven chapters (56-66) comes from various authors, most of whom wrote after the return from exile in 538 B.C.

A storm of protest broke loose. First it was Moses, the confidant of God and the inspired lawgiver; now the greatest of the inspired prophets also is the target of the critics. Duhm very soberly affirmed that a prophet is a sane, sensible man who has a message for contemporaries. What use did they have for descriptions of a situation which would not appear until a hundred and fifty years later? And what was the import for them of a Messiah in a still more remote future?

Precisely in this sober seriousness the believers in the church saw proof that the new school to which Duhm belonged had completely broken with the Christian faith. After all, one of the foundations of the faith lay in the fulfillment of prophecy. The new view of the book of Isaiah denied even the possibility of prophecy, as knowledge, given by God, of future events. It is true that Duhm did not make this point explicitly in his writing, but the believers who picked up his hefty book said that the denial of the supernatural could easily be read between the lines.

On June 28, 1908, the papal Biblical Commission responded with an "Answer" to some *dubia* which had been presented to it. Since this text is somewhat shorter than that of the preceding year on the Pentateuch, I shall give here a sample in translation for the interested reader who is willing to struggle with long sentences.

Dubium I
> Is it permissible to teach that the predictions which appear in the book of Isaiah — and elsewhere in the Scriptures — are not genuine predictions, but that they are stories which were invented after the events or, if it must be acknowledged that something was announced before it happened, that the prophet did not announce this in advance on the basis of a supernatural revelation from God who knows the future, but on the basis of what he conjectured, thanks to a fortuitous discernment and his own keenness of understanding?

Answer: No.

Dubium II
> Can one combine the thesis according to which Isaiah and other prophets spoke only of events of their own time or about things which would happen not long thereafter with the certain fact of the predictions which have to do with the Messiah and the events of the end, which the same prophets wrote far in advance, and with the general consensus of the church fathers who unanimously assure us that the prophets also predicted these things which must be fulfilled many centuries later?

Answer: No.

Dubium III
> Can one assume that the prophets, who not only

reproved human wickedness and proclaimed the word of God for the benefit of their hearers, but also predicted future events, always necessarily had to speak not to men in the future but to contemporaries who were present in order to be able fully to be understood by them; and that consequently the second part of the book of Isaiah (40-66), in which the seer does not address and offer comfort to men of Judah of Isaiah's time but Jews who are sorrowing in the Babylonian exile as though he lives among them, cannot have been written by Isaiah himself, who then was long since dead, but that it must be attributed to an unknown prophet who lived among the exiles?

Answer: No.

Dubium IV

Must one give such weight to the linguistic argument from word-usage and style, which serves to dispute the unity of the author of the book of Isaiah, that it compels a serious person, proficient in criticism and in the Hebrew language, to assume a multiple authorship for that book?

Answer: No.

Dubium V

Are there solid arguments which, when one takes them together with each other, incontestably prove that the book of Isaiah must be attributed not to Isaiah alone but to two or even more authors?

Answer: No.

With this the Catholic biblical scholars saw their investigations restricted to their inner chambers. If anyone was asked, for example, to write something about the development of the messianic expectations in the Old Testament, he found himself compelled to employ strange constructions. After the messianic picture of Isaiah (approximately 740-700 B. C.) he treated that of Jeremiah (approximately 627-586), then that of Ezekiel (after 593). He had to give corresponding treatment to the picture of the future that Isaiah (740-700) had sketched for the exiles in Babylon when Cyrus had appeared on the stage (after 550)....

Catholics who wanted to publish something about the much discussed questions concerning "the servant of the Lord" who appears in chapters 42, 49, 50, 52, 53, and 61 in the book of Isaiah had to express themselves, for example, in this fashion: "(According to the Biblical Commission) Isaiah experienced, in the spirit, the time of the exile, and he addresses himself to the exiles of the future as though he lived among them. Thus in the interpretation of these chapters we can take into account the special circumstances of the exile, which Isaiah had in view when these chapters were written."

Instruction along these lines was given also to the priests in all the seminaries throughout the world. I still remember very well how in 1937 we protested against the untruthfulness of that instruction: "Our professor himself does not believe what he is telling us."

In the Gereformeerde Kerken it was a different matter. There there was no papal Biblical Commission, and no apparatus for keeping a watchful eye on the seminaries. But there was the authority, much stronger because it was internal, of the belief in the divine inspiration. In his book of 1952, mentioned above, Aalders defends the authorship of Isaiah, on the traditional grounds. Among these grounds, for him, are those references in the New Testament which are explicitly attributed to the prophet himself, and not merely to the book which bears his name. Of course Aalders is familiar with all the arguments of modern criticism. Like the papal Biblical Commission in 1908, he finds that they are not convincing. The narrative chapters 36-39 can very well have been written by Isaiah himself. The emergence in chapter 40 of all sorts of new conceptions and ideas still is no indication of a new author. "This is all the more convincing when a person in full seriousness takes into account the fact that here *we are not dealing merely with purely human concepts but with Divine revelation.* There is no reason at all why God should not have imparted to one and the same prophet, at different periods of his prophetic activity, a different content of the revelation." The change in language and style proves nothing: "A writer would have to be poor in language indeed if he did not use terms and manners of expression in one case which he would omit using in other pieces from his pen."

Finally, it is characteristic of prophecy that it likes to describe what is coming as though it were already present. Isaiah could have realized as already present the destruction and exile which would come about much later, and could have known the Persian ruler Cyrus by name when his own contemporaries were not yet even aware that Persians existed. "'But,' some will say to us, 'is it likely that such a transporting in the spirit into a distant future as though it were already present would be maintained in so large a number of chapters?' To this it must be answered that it is true that we do not have another example of anything of this kind; *but why should we claim the right to place limitations on God's Spirit?* Is this Spirit not powerful enough that what he has repeatedly done with other prophets on a small scale he could accomplish with Isaiah on a grand scale?"

God indeed *can* do anything. He *can* let a person see and experience a situation of a hundred and fifty years later, and cause him to write words which fit perfectly into this situation. But why should he?

On a first reading of Isaiah 40-55 one notes that the prophet is constantly in conversation with his hearers, and again and again he responds to their reactions. But he cannot be a messenger from God who really lived among the exiles. This is not allowed, because of the dogma of inspiration and the historical reliability of the Bible. Who is it really who is placing limitations on the Spirit of God?

3. Chronicles: history and "fables"

I refer the reader to a specialist in cultural history for an answer to this question: in what period did people begin to think that a biblical story is true only if it gives a faithful recounting of facts? It seems to me that this narrowing of the concept entered only after the Middle Ages. In any case, it led to great difficulties when historical criticism arose. The practitioners of this critical study showed that much of what is related in the Scripture cannot have happened in this way. In response to this they were informed from the side of believers that they were misled by their prejudices: "You think, in your pride, that God (if you even believe in his existence) cannot intervene in this world; thus that he can do no miracles and cannot reveal to men what will happen long after their own times; therefore you say that certain biblical stories cannot be true." Believers who were better informed on the matter found this response inadequate. They knew that the Bible sometimes relates the same event in two sharply different ways. These two accounts cannot both be true. Must one then acknowledge that one of them is incorrect? But this is impossible for someone who accepts the divine inspiration and with it the inerrancy of the Bible, the utter absence of any error. What then must he do with the conflicting reports?

I choose Chronicles as an example of a biblical book which more than once has put believing readers in this difficult position. The arrangement of this historical work is very simple:

I Chronicles 1-9   genealogies (beginning with Adam)
                10-29 the reign of David
II Chronicles 1-9 the reign of Solomon
                10-36 the reigns of the kings of Judah

It appears from this plan that the interest of the writer is directed to David, his son Solomon, and all the successors in his dynasty down to the fall of Jerusalem. Now in the course of his narrative he cites all sorts of sources from which he has taken his material. They are usually "prophecies," "visions," or "books" which bear the name of a prophet; sometimes they also are a "book of the kings of Judah" and a "commentary (*midrash*) on the book of kings." None of these documents has been preserved for us, unless these last two named are our biblical books of Samuel and Kings. It is certain that the writer of Chronicles had these books, or a revision of them, before him when he wrote his own work. Any reader of the Bible can ascertain this for himself if he will place beside Chronicles the corresponding texts in Samuel and Kings. But then he also encounters difficulties. Chronicles often gives a version which is quite different.

The best known example is the account of the census which David had made at God's command and for which he was punished by an epidemic among his people. He bought the threshing-floor of Araunah just outside Jerusalem and Araunah's oxen for fifty shekels of silver. When he had an altar built there, upon which he offered the oxen, God caused the plague to cease.

This story from II Samuel 24 is told in I Chronicles 21 with striking differences. Here it is Satan who prompts David to conduct the census. David sees the destroying angel and his drawn sword. He is more generous toward Araunah (here spelled Ornan) and gives him six hundred golden shekels. The sacrificial animals are consumed by a fire that comes from heaven.

In cases like this one can try to show that there actually are no differences: one "harmonizes" the texts, as it is called. Or one says that both accounts are dependent upon an older account with many more details, which were appropriated in one way by one writer and in another way by the other. Or one finds still other ways to eliminate the repugnant idea that there is something in the Scripture that does not ring true. God alone knows how much time, energy, and ingenuity is devoted to this kind of effort to render secure the "truth" of the Bible.

In 1939 a German commentary on Chronicles appeared, written by a Catholic biblical scholar. This work was regarded as setting the tone for many years to come. The writer says that the question of the historical reliability of Chronicles forms a special difficulty for "the Bible-believing interpreters, especially the Catholics, for whom the inerrancy (the absence of any error) of every historical work in the Bible is fixed, as a matter of principle." With overpowering erudition, which renders so many pages of this bulky volume almost unreadable, the writer bravely goes into all the historical difficulties; but often he must concede that they "cannot be solved at the moment." In the case of David's sacrifice just cited, he takes refuge in the assumption of a common source for the two stories: the writer of II Samuel is supposed to have omitted the reference to the heavenly fire, which was reported in I Chronicles, because he "preferred a less expressive description."

The encyclical *Divino afflante* of 1943 also had a liberating effect with respect to the Chronicles. The Biblical Commission had not given explicit attention to this book. But it was covered by the second "Answer" which the Commission issued in June 1905: one must not all too easily assume that biblical narratives which give the impression of offering genuine history in fact intend to give a parable or something of that sort, and not hard facts. Catholic defenders of the inerrancy of the Bible had tried to take this route. Shortly before this the Commission had likewise cut off another route. Its first "Answer" dealt with the so-called implicit citations. Where the inspired writer tells an improbable story, some would say that without saying so (implicitly) he was quoting a source or an authority without accepting responsibility for that report himself. Thus Catholic interpreters of the Bible had tried to preserve the inspiration; in this way improbable things and contradictions could be charged to the account of others than the inspired writer himself. No, the Commission said, this approach is possible only when one can show that the sacred writer in fact was quoting, and that he himself clearly dissociated himself from what he quoted.

All these tortuous devices were rendered superfluous in 1943. Then Catholic interpreters could with an easy conscience take their places in company with the practitioners of "historical criticism." In the meantime, in these circles the assessment of Chronicles had undergone sharp change since Wellhausen. As a child of his time, Wellhausen had expressed himself haughtily and scornfully about the writer, the Chronicler, for whom religion appeared to consist entirely of the externals of the liturgy, and who appeared to press God into the straitjacket of a strict retribution. In order to prove his unworthy views, he seemed to have manipulated good historical documents, and that without any artistic skill. A tedious falsifier of history: this is what the judgment amounted to. More recent criticism recognized, on the one hand, the historical reliability of a number of items of information in Chronicles, as a valuable supplement to what is handed down in Kings. On the other hand, it acquired an appreciation for the way in which the Chronicler had given form to the insights of faith and the expectations which thrived in his milieu. This appreciation very soon became common property among Catholics, partly because it was expressed in translations of the Bible which were intended for the ordinary church people. One of these translations says that the Chronicler sometimes hands down reliable historical material, but there are times when he "gives facts at variance with the account offered by Samuel and Kings, or when he even deliberately modifies these accounts. This would be unforgivable in a historian of today whose job is to narrate and explain the sequence of events. But the author of Chronicles has no such intention. He is not a historian; he is a theologian. Contemplating the long history of Israel and particularly the Davidic episode, he paints a picture of the ideal kingdom. Past, present and future merge into one; into the age of David he projects the actual organizatin of his own, omits all that might diminish his hero, David, who for him is the type of the longed-for messianic king. Apart from certain fresh items of information, the value of which must be independently tested, the work is not so much a record of the past as a picture of the conditions and interests of the author's own period."

This approach no longer has any problem with the six hundred shekels of gold which the Chronicler has David paying for the threshing-floor. According to experts on biblical monetary values, this is about two hundred times the amount that II Samuel has David paying, the fifty shekels of silver. For the Chronicler is concerned about the temple which was built on the site of the threshing-floor, and for him David is the model of generosity when it is a matter of worship that is involved. Therefore he has him giving an enormous amount of gold for this sacred plot instead of buying it with silver. The amount becomes six hundred shekels of gold. For, once again contrary to the account in II Samuel, the Chronicler has David ruling from the very first over all twelve tribes; therefore he multiplies the number fifty in his source by twelve. Indeed he believes that in the last analysis it was not David who destined the threshing-floor to be the site of the temple; it was God himself. He expresses that belief in old biblical terms with the fire that falls from heaven, a miraculous bolt of lightning that consumes David's burnt offering, and that he also adduces later on in the story of the dedication of the temple by Solomon.

For one who holds to the orthodox confessions this approach is still unacceptable. Aalders, who is very well acquainted with the new appreciation of Chronicles, expressed this clearly: "Such an evaluation of Chronicles is squarely in conflict with our point of departure, that the Old Testament, as part of the Bible, is the infallible Word of God, of which we declare, in agreement with Article 4 of our

Dutch Confession of Faith: 'We believe without any doubt all that is contained in it.'" This forces him into the use of tortuous devices such as we described above. Thus he thinks that he can bring the different amounts of money in the threshing-floor story closer together by conceiving of the shekels in Chronicles as "round metal discs of much less weight."

It is true that anyone who dismisses the principle of the perfect historical accuracy of the biblical stories frees himself from many difficulties, but then he encounters others, of a more serious nature. One of these had to do with the scope of the Bible. Toward the end of the first century of the Christian era the rabbis in Palestine arrived at a narrow restriction of the sacred books. They excluded from these a number of pious writings which however were counted in the holy Scriptures by Jews throughout the world who read Greek. Because the Christians used the Jewish Bible in the Greek form, they too included in it some pious writings which the rabbis in Palestine had excluded.

Among the church fathers it was primarily the scholars who took these differences into account. Jerome lived in Bethlehem and took lessons from rabbis. Engaged in the task of translating the Bible into good Latin for the benefit of the Roman church, he felt some hesitation when it came time to deal with these books which according to his Jewish teachers did not belong to the holy Scripture. Yet, as he says in the foreword to Tobit, he finally submitted to the general feeling of the Church rather than to the insights of the rabbis.

The Reformation was dominated by the theme, at that time very clear, of "back to the sources." It could accept as books of the Old Testament only those writings which also were recognized among the Jews as Bible. Thus it came to the denial of the inspired character of the others, which were given the name of "the Apocrypha." The synod of Dort, which in 1618 reached the decision to make a new Dutch translation of the Bible, shrank, however, from leaving these apocrypha entirely out of the forthcoming *Statenbijbel*. If they had done so, the Dutch churches would thereby have broken step with the Anglican and Lutheran churches in the other countries, who had held to the Bible in its former scope. Therefore it was decided to provide a place for the Apocrypha in an appendix, after the last book of the New Testament, with separate pagination, set in less attractive type, without marginal notes, and preceded by a "Waerschouwinge aan de Lesers" ("warning to the readers"). In this warning arguments were given as to why these apocryphal books could not be holy Scripture. The most explicit reason is the proof that they contain "untrue, absurd, fabulous, and contradictory matters," which are not in harmony with the truth nor with the real biblical books.

Anyone who now agrees that some stories in Chronicles stem entirely or in part from the pious imagination must then ask himself whether he still has reason to exclude from the Bible such books as Tobit and Judith. To give a single example: the story of II Chronicles 20 now is seen as an expression of the belief that the strength and the salvation of the Jewish community are dependent upon prayer and praise. After the moving prayer of king Jehoshaphat, representative of the nation, and the exhortation of a prophet, the forces of Judah go forth to meet the innumerable hosts of the three armies that were marching against them. In their front ranks march the Levites, attired in their liturgical garments. As soon as they catch sight of the enemy, they begin to praise the Lord with a loud voice. The enemy armies immediately turn their weapons against each other, and the Jews have nothing to do but to carry away the spoil from among the corpses, a task that requires three days. Anyone who recognizes that it is the primary aim of the Chronicler here to portray the faith of his community and therewith to strengthen it cannot adduce any further objections in principle against the "inspiration" of a writing like the book of Judith.

4. Loss of the old certainties

In the course of 1963 a minister friend of mine telephoned me. "Say, you are so much at home in the spelling of old placenames in the Bible and such, will you help me?" He had undertaken to translate a book that described excavations in the biblical lands. When I asked him what the book was, he gave me the title: "Und die Bibel hat doch Recht" ("And the Bible is right after all"; the book appeared in English under the title, *The Bible as History*). I had never heard of it, and hence at once became furious: "What a swindle! what a rotten title!" After talking about it back and forth I promised him my help under one condition: he would see to it that the Dutch edition got a different title. Of course I should have considered the fact that as translator he could not possibly enforce this condition. No publisher would abandon such a lure as this title.

But I was just that angry about the title. I had participated in excavations in Palestine often enough to know what visitors expected by way of "proofs" of the trustworthiness of the Bible. And I knew how journalists misused what we told them, and particularly what we did not tell them, in order to satisfy the wishes of their readers. So as soon as I heard this title I knew what kind of book it had to be: a collection of obsolete data, covered with the sauce of a fresh journalistic style, with the aim of comforting the dear believers in their uncertainty. They hear from the modern interpreters that the Bible is full of untruths. "What you always believed in your heart but did not dare to express for fear of appearing old-fashioned, — now you can come out with it once again; I shall prove from archaeology that the Bible is right after all...."

Hundreds of thousands of copies of the book were sold in

several languages. Insofar as scholars in the field took any notice of it, they severely criticized it. So great is the cleft still which we have seen identified already around 1840 by Lutz, a cleft between the biblical scholars on the one hand and the church people on the other. In a Swiss theological journal of 1956 one may read something that sounds like an echo of Wellhausen's complaint of 1842: "I am rather rendering my hearers unfit for the ecclesiastical office." There it involved a preacher for whom the biblical stories about Abraham are not historical. "In view of his pastoral and ecclesiastical responsibility he will be able openly to declare his convictions only with pain and fear. For apart from the fact that he will plunge the flock entrusted to him into grave doubt and will not be pointing them to the way to the firm stay in life which they need, he will be conscious that he is surrendering the form and content of the entire Bible to a process of erosion, as soon as he denies the historicity — and therewith the truth — of so important a part of the Bible. The theologian with a sense of responsibility, who in his intellectual honesty thinks that he must give credence to this conclusion, can at the most seek his deliverance in an attempt so far as possible to remain silent about the existence of the Abraham stories. Thus we know pastors who never preach about Abraham or use his history in their instruction in the faith."

To complete this chapter I shall attempt briefly and concisely, and therefore without laboring over fine distinctions, to state some of the questions and doubts which the historical approach has evoked, beginning with the Old Testament.

Thanks to excavations and textual studies our knowledge of the world in which ancient Israel lived has greatly increased since the end of the last century. Yet the concrete figures of Israel's patriarchs remain veiled in the darkness. According to the best experts on this period of oriental history, they will always remain so, considering the nature of the biblical narratives. This holds true for Moses and the Exodus, and just as much so for the earliest history of Israel's tribes in Canaan.

We have seen how sharply the Bible-believers reacted to the new approach, particularly when Wellhausen presented it so convincingly. They felt that he actually placed the entire doctrine of inspiration in doubt, and with it the entirety of the Christian faith. This feeling grew still stronger when people in the church later began to place the emphasis upon "the historical character of the revelation." God reveals himself, so it was said, in and through facts. The terms "salvation-history" and "facts of salvation" came into use everywhere. Hence the old question was posed in a new form: what can there be of revelation to us in facts of which we do not know the true nature? The promise to Abraham, Moses, the Exodus, the revelation at Sinai, the conquest of the Promised Land, — of just these fundamental facts of salvation the scholars say that there is nothing left to be said with certainty.

One attitude, of course, is to accuse these scholars of fostering doubt, and in spite of them to hold fast to the "historical kernel" in these saving facts. Another is not to call the facts themselves revelatory, but the stories about them which Israel related and wrote down. In this case it is the faith of Israel that is "revelatory," and then what actually happened does not become an issue. But then what becomes of the God who works in history?

Still another difficulty appeared no less serious. The historical approach included the attempt to understand the ancient texts in terms of their own time. They were placed, as it were, back in their original milieu. The question with which one approached the text was always this: what did the man who wrote this down at that time intend to say? This way of working had to lead to the difficulty: what then are we doing with that book from before Christ's time? In him, after all, the earlier revelation came to a climax which was never thereafter to be surpassed. Why then is this ballast of the incomplete pre-history still dragged along?

In the second century of our era the scholar Marcion had proposed to the churches that they drop the Old Testament entirely, and of the New to keep only those parts which bore witness to the "alien" God of love who had become manifest in Jesus. When modern criticism had placed the ancient biblical texts back in their original milieu, the very same proposal was made by a great German scholar. Wellhausen and those of a kindred mind had, without saying so explicitly, studied the Old Testament as the document of an ancient religion, actually not differently from the way in which scholars in the field of religions analyzed texts of other ancient religions. The German scholar referred to, Adolf von Harnack, wrote in 1920, in a large-scale study of Marcion, that the maintenance of the Old Testament by the Protestant churches in the present time could only be seen as the consequence of a religious and ecclesiastical paralysis.

Thus the Nazis found support among Christian theologians when, in their hatred for all that was Jewish, they tried to make the Old Testament, as a product of "the inferior Jewish mind," a forbidden book. A reaction promptly came from the Christian side: in 1934 Wilhelm Vischer published a book with the expressive title "Het Christusgetuigenis van het Oude Testament" (German title, "Das Christuszeugnis des Alten Testaments," English translation, "The Witness to Christ in the Old Testament"). According to this interpretation, the centuries-old interpretation of the Christians, the imperishable value of the ancient book lay in the fact that it bears witness to Christ. But how? Following the church fathers, all the succeeding generations had assumed that the inspiring Spirit had placed in these ancient texts meanings which were hidden from the Jews, but which he now made clear to the members of Christ's church. But this way of reading them had become impossible for modern Christians. This was true first of all because they could no longer believe in this form of inspiration, and consequently because the expositions of the church fathers appeared to them to be utterly arbitrary mosaic work. Still a search is steadily under way for answers to the problem hereby raised. The great Rudolf Bultmann has proposed that we regard the Old Testament as the history of a failure. He shows that all the efforts to actualize a right relationship to God in a community on this earth come to nought. Thus the Old Testament is "prophecy" through its own inner contradiction. And thus a reading from that ancient book can make clear to the Christian which road he must not take. According to Bultmann the same thing can be made clear to him also by other, "profane" texts and by encounters and incidents in his life as well. Other theologians have found this approach too negative, however. But they still have not found an unequivocal answer to give to the question of what role that ancient book then does have to fill in the Christian churches.

"What then must become of the New Testament if people begin to apply these theories to the gospels as well?" To my amazement I read this sentence in the conclusion to a little book which the Jesuit scholar Leopold Fonck published in Innsbruck in 1905. According to the title he had described "the battle over the truth of the Holy Scriptures in the past twenty-five years." Did he not know then that this application of which he wrote had already been in process for almost a century? Or did he mean its penetration into "the Roman Catholic camp"? In any case, one finds nothing in his book about Reimarus, whose writings were published by the great Lessing beginning in 1794. These writings marked the beginning in Germany of the passionately pursued search for "the historical Jesus." When as a child of the Enlightenment one can no longer believe in supernatural things such as revelation or the inspiration of the Bible, and in dogmas like that of the incarnation, what then was the actual life of Jesus and what significance can it still have for us modern men? In 1902 Albert Schweitzer published a survey of that study, the "quest of the historical Jesus" from Reimarus, mentioned above, to the work of the biblical scholar Wrede, which had appeared just the preceding year, on "the messianic secret in the gospel of Mark." While Schweitzer took his own route, Wrede later appeared to be one of the pioneers in the method of "form criticism." Beginning in the 1920's, this approach to the gospels began to dominate the field of research. Like Moses, now Jesus also, in his person and his work, seemed to disappear in the mist of uncertainties; the new scientific study of the gospels showed that they only bear witness to the faith of the infant church, and that it is no longer possible to go behind these testimonies to the historical appearance of Jesus.

In 1966 these uncertainties led to a sharp conflict in Germany. Orthodox church leaders called for a protest. While earlier people talked about a steadily widening cleft between the biblical scholars and the Bible-believing people, now signs pointed to a "yawning chasm." It no longer appeared possible to bridge this chasm. "On March 6, 1966, with the sound of a thousand trumpets was begun the battle of the congregations against the professors using biblical criticism, the battle concerning Jesus, concerning his words and miracles, concerning belief in the virgin birth and the resurrection. Twenty-two thousand Protestants filled the Westfalenhalle in Dortmund for a great rally which was, in fact, a combination heresy-trial and prayer-meeting." For the editors of the weekly newspagazine, *Der Spiegel,* the case was sensational enough to justify devoting very particular attention to it. They published a series of articles in which the numerous differences of opinion among leading German theologians on the most important points of belief concerning Jesus were strongly emphasized. The last article ended in a thoroughly journalistic fashion. The writer quoted a sentence from Luther in which he refers to Jesus' promise that he will be with his disciples until the end of the world. Then he has the same certainty of faith expressed by a modern theologian: "It is He, [Jesus,] who preserves the church." The concluding line which the writer added to this consisted of only two words: "Which Jesus?"

There is indeed a way to avoid all these uncertainties. Some people unite in a group from which the new approach is carefully excluded. "We hold fast to the confession and we believe without any doubt all that stands in the Holy Scripture...." In the Netherlands this has led to separation and then to further separation from the separated group. Shortly after the war I visited in Kampen with a professor who taught Old Testament. It did not surprise me that he vigorously argued to prove Moses' authorship of the Pentateuch. But I did feel cold chills when he showed me a pamphlet from his own hand which identified the synodal church, from which his group had separated, with the great harlot of the book of Revelation. There was something chilling about the certainty of conviction with which his small group felt itself to be the only true church of Christ, with the exclusion of all others throughout the entire world. The earlier-mentioned Poels had written, in 1898, in the style then common, about "the little mother who always sits at the same window with her knitting. For her this one street is the world. She has never seen the Alps. For her there is nothing higher than the spires in her little village. This dear soul thinks that the big clock at which she just now is looking through the eternally drawn curtains tells time for all mankind under God's sun. And ah! our little knitting mother does not sit alone! People who know how to remove the church are peering through the same window...." This was intended for Catholics who did not want to hear of a new approach. Even in a worldwide church fellowship the maintaining of old certainties can be a sign of narrowness of mind and spirit.

The most extreme example of this is provided by the Jehovah's witnesses, who are represented in almost all the countries of the world. The members must believe in the inspiration of the Bible in the strictest sense of the word.

Corresponding to this is a system of "exposition" which is equally obligatory and is regularly prescribed for all the groups throughout the world from the center. The posing of critical questions arises out of "the spirit of the evil world." Becoming a member of the company signifies that one abandons all connections with this world. This is quite correctly seen; for to them it is true that anyone who raises questions and admits doubts can no longer bear witness.

3

From Impasse To Oecumene

It appears that there are only two ways to get out of the impasse. One is to hold fast to the old doctrine of inspiration and thus to the divine authority of the Bible. Then we shall also remain faithful to the old formulations, the confessions and doctrinal statements of the church which express this belief and are based upon it. And in our believing thinking about the Bible we shall simply refuse to admit human views which could attack these certainties. This is the way of clearly-stated doctrine, with clear marks which narrowly define the boundaries between belief and unbelief. It is also the way of the clearly delineated group, church, or — if one will — sect.

Or we may choose without reservation for the historical approach. We analyze the Bible with the methods of study which in our time are applied to any other ancient book. What appears therein by way of supernatural events, "acts of God," miracles, prophecies, we see as expressions of faith of people who had a world-view different from our own. The Bible then contains no objective divine revelation. In itself it has no more authority than any other book of religion. This is the way of unrestrained modernism. Subjective opinions take the place of objective truths. There is no more common ground to point to, upon which together we can form a group, church or sect. This way inevitably leads to the dissolution of the existing churches and ultimately of Christianity.

In this chapter I should like to describe a third possibility, a kind of middle way which is being taken by more and more Christians. They have unreservedly chosen the historical approach, but they combine this with a stance which in their view fully merits the name of faith. According to them this way leads to a new common appreciation and experience of what the Bible is really all about, and this has *everything* to do with what is denoted in the word "Oecumene."

Of course in this short span I cannot give more than a sketch. As preamble, a couple of remarks, the significance of which perhaps will become clear only after further reading.

1. A new climate

At the end of December 1964 the "Society for Biblical Literature and Exegesis" met in New York in a more festive gathering than was common. This was the one hundredth meeting since the founding of the Society in 1880. The book in which the papers presented there are bound points to its ecumenical character. Scholars from many countries, from Protestant, Roman Catholic, and Jewish circles, participated. "Perhaps the most amazing conclusion to which some readers will come is that the agreements among writers outnumber their disagreements."

No biblical scholar is surprised at this. For him it is taken for granted that he keeps up with the research done by all his colleagues in his field, at conventions and congresses when he has time and money for them, but always in the scholarly journals. In biblical research it usually can hardly be discerned from which church or confession a participant comes. This too is unimportant. What matters is his argumentation. Of course, the study of the meaning of ancient texts is not a mathematics. It knows nothing of the certainty of mathematical proofs. For it is a historical study; there the force of an argument can depend in part on capacity for empathy, on deeply rooted preconceptions and the like, which are conditioned by temperament and education, and even by an ecclesiastical milieu. But in genuine discussion even all this can freely be laid out on the table and discussed.

To summarize: *the practice of biblical scholarship brings together people from various nations and churches, in a spirit of objective research.* This also leads, where needed, to their beginning to take a more historical approach to the claims of their own church or confession.

An example may serve to make this clear. In Matthew 16 stands the saying of Jesus, "Thou art Peter, and upon this rock I will build my church." Since the Reformation the meaning of this saying has been a point of contention. In the dispute it never was doubted that Jesus had uttered this promise thus, on a particular day, in the vicinity of Caesarea Philippi. The interconfessional argument sometimes took on the character of a "yes-it-is-no-it-isn't" quarrel, in which everyone decided from the perspective of his own thought-world what the text must or must not mean.

Anything of that sort now has become impossible. A historical approach begins with the person who wrote the text. That is the author of the first gospel, identified by the name Matthew. An analysis is made of the style of writing and the use of language of this author, and of the manner in which he arranged the material which he had at his disposal. Did that material include the gospel of Mark? It appears that Matthew has inserted the promise of Jesus into mark's narrative, as an answer to Peter's confession, which he, Matthew has inserted the promise of Jesus into Mark's God." Why did Matthew do this, and why just at this point? Other than in this passage, the word *ekklesia*, church or community, appears only one time in the four gospels, and that is a little later in Matthew, in chapter 18; there it stands in a saying of Jesus that very clearly bears Matthew's stamp. Did Jesus in fact speak about his future *ekklesia*? If so, must that not have been just before his passion, or afterwards, as the Risen One? And what did he have in mind in doing so?

These are far from being the only questions which the text evokes. It appears to me unlikely that the participants in the research on this matter ever think about the papacy, either for or against it. As far as they are concerned, that lies in an entirely different order of things, even if they are not aware that the gospel text in question came to be used in this sharpened sense only in the course of the centuries (not yet by Augustine, as we have seen earlier).

To take still another example: since the Reformation people have come to understand Paul from the perspective of the personal struggle of Luther, which was extremely closely connected with the experience of faith of his time. Thus people began to have Paul saying all sorts of things about sin, law, and grace which he did not intend, and could not have meant. For preoccupation with one's own conscience was something that became customary only some centuries later, in the western sector of the church. The recognition of this fact can provide a new vision of what Paul did mean, and, for example, also of the question whether the heart of the gospel is correctly identified as "justification by faith." It was encouraging that some years ago at Harvard, during a discussion between Catholic and Protestants, the influence of Luther and his time upon the interpretation of Paul was brought forward by a Scandinavian scholar, one who was of the Lutheran persuasion.

Biblical research along this line can also lead to an ecumenical stance in still another way. It shows *that we do not have proclaimed in the Bible a doctrine, in the sense of a comprehensive whole of doctrinal theses.*

Jesus did not bring a new teaching in this sense. We saw this in the first chapter of this book. Where the New Testament attempts to put into words the significance of Christ's person and work, it seems that each writer in so doing takes the paths of his own thought, under greater or lesser influence of the thought of his environment. Therefore one cannot say that the New Testament affords us a particular doctrine about Christ, a "Christology." It has almost become a commonplace to say that there, various Christologies stand alongside each other, which cannot be reduced to the same denominator without doing violence to the thinkers and writers of the young church. This early church knew a pluriformity in her experience and confession which in later centuries is all too often forgotten. Anyone who says that he regards the New Testament as binding for the church will be obliged to accept and to cultivate such a pluriformity.

It is no different in the Old Testament. Often the suggestion is raised that this collection of books is dominated by one and the same view of Israel's history, "salvation-history." B. van Iersel recently pointed out the many variations in the survey of salvation-history which the Bible offers. "Because of the variations, one cannot, in my opinion, speak of *the* history of salvation. And my position then is also that *the* history of salvation does not exist. What we do have are histories of salvation, in the plural. And there are many of these. The specific forms of these salvation-histories are strongly tied, on the one hand, to the literary context in which they appear, and on the other side also to the historical situation in which they function." Further, there are entire books which appear to know nothing of such a salvation-history. In Proverbs, Job, and Ecclesiastes the names of Israel and Jerusalem do not appear, nor do the concepts of covenant and election. Alongside the ecstatic rejoicing of believers who see God as overpoweringly active in particular facts, to which witness is borne by so many hymns in the book of Psalms and in the prophetic writings also, there are utterances by people who cannot discover any special activity of God in history at all. One may think of the Preacher in Ecclesiastes, and perhaps still more of the sage Agur in Proverbs 30. According to some translators the utterance of this man is supposed to have signified that he had become weary in his searching for the meaning of things. But there is much to argue that the utterance of Agur originally was, "There is no God, there is no God, and I am exhausted." It is understandable that this was too strong for the ancient copyists and translators of the text.

This brings me to the third preliminary remark. Among many Christians in our time one detects *a certain reluctance to use the word "God."* This could be connected with, and conducive of, an understanding and use of the Bible that is *less self-assured.*

It is as difficult for people to talk about God now as it was easy for them to do so earlier. Some find themselves embarrased or perplexed when they hear others speaking about God as though they were dealing with a well-known entity, something clearly delineated, something that you can define and that you can bring into your speaking and your reasoning whenever you will. The resistance to this use of the word "God" is not lessened when the Bible is cited in that connection. On the contrary, anyone who talks fluently about God in biblical terms can count on antipathy from an increasing number of people. "God has said this or that; God usually does thus and so; look at the ways of God; we admire and praise his great deeds which are written in his Word that we have here in our hands, this book, God's Word...."

Whence comes this increasing resistance to this kind of talk? Perhaps people are now concerned, more widely and more strongly than previously, over the fact that in the name of this clearly defined biblical God innumerable people are oppressed, mistreated, and killed. Charlemagne, who had thousands of Saxons slain because of their unbelief in his God, was not the first to do something of this sort, and alas! the soldiers of the Wehrmacht, who had "Gott mit uns" on their beltbuckles, were not the last. People do not understand a God who lets himself be put at the service of force and tyranny.

However that may be, a certain reserve in talking about God appears to be an advantage for a genuine contact with the people who speak in the Bible. This theme is regularly expressed in the Old Testament: anyone who has caught a glimpse of God must die. Thus the biblical men express the idea that God is overpoweringly different from man, so much so that in a genuine encounter with God, man would die. Of course, it is known that to a few was granted what can be called an "association with God." The most privileged among them was Moses, with whom according to Exodus 33 God spoke "face to face, as a man speaks with his fellow-man." But later in the same chapter it is related that God said to Moses: "You cannot see my face, for no man can see my face and live."

To the Corinthians, who were so keen for profound insights, Paul writes that in faith a sure knowledge of God is granted to us; that knowing, however, is only partial, and our speaking on the basis of this knowledge, however prophetic it may be, is only childish prattle.

There is, at the present time, a growing interest to be noted in the great figures who have known God, whom we call mystics. They bear witness, each in his or her own way, to the absolute otherness of God, who can only be known in the darkness of faith. The great personages among "those who talk about God," whom we call theologians, confirm this. In Thomas Aquinas' work we find utterances such as these: "We have some knowledge of God only by knowing what he is not." "The better we come to know God in this life, the better we comprehend that he is above all that can be grasped by the understanding." When this theologian was seized by a fatal illness on his way to a council in 1274, he was reading the Song of Solomon, that favorite book of Christian mystics since Origen.

Along with other factors, an increasing realization of the mystery of existence that is called "God" will make it increasingly difficult for Christians to withdraw and to (continue to) form closed groups with slogans such as "We possess the truth" or "The pure faith is to be found only with us."

2. Israel: "the divine" founds a fellowship

What we have called in the foregoing sections "the historical approach" could also be called "taking a detached view." The biblical scholars of the last century detached themselves from a life of the church in which the Bible held a central position. It was believingly viewed and experienced as the word through which God ever anew addresses men in the here-and-now. By taking their distance from that view, they created the possibility of comparing the religion of ancient Israel with those of the surrounding nations. In this way what was distinctive about Israel's religion could come into focus.

In one of his discriminating little books Romano Guardini once described how one can conceive that situation in which, according to the experts, the phenomenon of religion has its origin. They call it "the religious experience." In his account, Guardini tells of the experience of a friend: "He was walking alone through a forest and came to an open place. It was midday and everything was filled with the profound quiet that can prevail at that hour. It was utterly still, no birds sang, nothing was moving. The warmth of the sun filled the area without stirring. Suddenly, he said, he was seized by a profound uneasiness. It was not fright, such as can be caused by something in particular, for example by an animal or by the feeling that another person is present, but something entirely different without any obvious cause, inexpressible, but so irresistible and overpowering that he ran away blindly, until he finally stopped, utterly exhausted and trembling all over. The narrator had experienced what the Greeks called the fear of Pan, 'panic.'

Now let us just imagine that this had not happened in our twentieth century, but in the seventh or eighth century before

Christ; and not in a wooded area maintained by experienced foresters, but in a lonely primeval forest of Asia Minor or northern Greece; and that the narrator himself was not a scientifically educated man of our time, but a herdsman who lived with his flock; and that he had something of what can be called religious genius, visionary power, the capacity to experience religious mystery and to express it in forms, — then he might have seen a strange being sitting on a boulder: half man and half animal, with terrifying eyes and pointed ears, and a powerful force had emanated from this being, terror and attraction at the same time, both fascination and fear. Then this herdsman would have run to his comrades and said, 'A god has appeared to me!' And they would have called him Pan, the god of nature that is both familiar and alien, both alluring and terrifying.

We can imagine the rise of the conceptions of the gods as occurring in something like this fashion. People of an earlier time, who did not have a critical attitude toward things of life, but were directly open to them, experienced the mystery that is revealed in the world immediately around them and that yet led further, deeper, that bestows upon the world a special significance and at the same time causes it to be wrapped up in the ineffable. Moreover, they had the ability to see it, not abstractly, but in images; in this way it was enacted for them in figures and happenings."

After this Guardini describes how the great realities in nature, such as sun, earth, sea, and wind, become gods, figures whose deeds and fates are related in the kind of narratives that we call "myths."

Something of this sort must also lie at the beginning of Israel's religion, an overpowering experience of the mystery that lies behind things, and a narrative in which that divine reality appears in action. The Bible has preserved only later formulations of all this. Taking our point of departure here, we may perhaps say the following: the founders of Israel's religion must have experienced the mystery of existence, more strongly than was true elsewhere, as a "someone." The attracting aspect about this experience then must have consisted in the fact that the mystery which was presented as personal disclosed itself as saving, as bestowing existence. The aspect that evoked fear then came to expression in the absoluteness and the inescapable character of its claims. But equally characteristic was the fact that it did not "claim" those affected as separate individuals, but with an eye to their group. Thus it was a religious experience in which the mystery of existence was overpoweringly presented as "personality," as seeking relationship, as establishing a community.

A story was coupled with this experience also. But the mystery did not appear in it in a concrete form. This "personality" was indicated with a name, with the four consonants *Jhwh*. As to the origin and meaning of this name nothing can (yet?) be said with any uncertainty. The ancient Israelites used it very freely. But in the last centuries before Christ the Jews began to avoid it. Where it appeared in the sacred texts, they read another word, "the Lord," and in utterances and writings they usually used paraphrases, such as "heaven," "the name," "the power," "the dwelling" (in the temple), and the like. In this way the ancient pronounciation of *Jhwh* fell into forgetfulness. It probably was pronounced "Yahweh," but that is not certain. In his famous German translation of the Bible Martin Buber very fittingly chose the personal pronoun as his rendering of *Jhwh*. One may compare the following arbitrarily chosen words from the Psalms in the usual translation —

Sing to *the Lord* a new song...
It is good to praise *the Lord*...
How great are thy works, O *Lord*!
with Buber's version:
Singt *Ihm* einen neuen Gesang...
Gut ist es, *Dir* zu danken...
Wie gross sind deine Taten, Du!

(Sing to *him* a new song...
It is good to give thanks to *thee*...
How great are thy deeds, *thou!*).

The story is not enacted either wholly or in part in higher spheres, in a supraterrestrial, divine world, but entirely on this earth. A group of slaves had made an effort to escape from Egypt. At a critical moment they escaped the danger of total annihilation. "He" had done this. In this way He had made this group his own people. Israel knew that it existed by the grace of his saving act. It would not even be if He had not intervened, out of pure compassion for oppressed people. Therefore it always repeated, in praise and prayer, his name, his own name, written out in full: "He who led us out of Egypt."

Herewith the foundation was laid for *a religion which is conspicuous among all others because of its attention to man*. The divine took on form, "revealed itself" through a deliverance out of the inhuman condition of slavery and through the creation of a society on the basis of a number of "human rights," unequivocally formulated as absolute demands, demands from God. I refer to the ancient formula of the "Ten Commandments." It has long been suggested that they are intended as two sets of five each, so that the Israelite could enumerate on ten fingers the fundamental "truths" of his faith. I do not know who made the suggestion, but it is an instructive one.

After God has introduced himself to his people, "I am Jahweh who led you out of Egypt," he sums up his claims. The Israelite may not acknowledge any other power alongside him. He must not make any image and thereby create for himself or for others the suggestion that in some sense he has Jahweh at his disposal. That would also be the implication if he were to use Jahweh's sacred name in heathen fashion as an instrument of magic. He must devote one day of the week, the Sabbath, to Jahweh; this is to acknowledge that actually all time, and thus the whole of existence, is from God, and to allow, for himself and for his fellowmen, rest from the hard work that is a reminder of the killing slave-labor in Egypt. Finally, he must honor his parents, through whom Jahweh gave him life. For parents are not ordinary fellowmen; they belong to the order of God.

One's actual fellowmen come up for discussion in the last five commandments, "thou shalt not kill," and so on. If we consider that "kill" in the text does not refer to killing in war or to the death penalty as the outcome of a judicial process, but willful murder, and further, that "steal" probably refers only to the robbing of a fellowman in order to make him a slave, and finally that "covet" in the ancient Hebrew includes the actual seizure of something, then it appears that Jahweh sets in a line with his own rights five fundamental rights of man, his rights to life, marriage, liberty, a good name, and possessions. One could count off the rights of God and the rights of one's fellowman on the fingers of the two hands, and these two hands fit together.

In texts such as Leviticus 19 we can see that in the person of Jahweh lies the real reason why one must do right to his fellowman, and more than that. The prescriptions for society are there interrupted again and again by the utterance, "I am Jahweh." He has made himself known as the deliverer from distress and through this saving act has called his people Israel into life. Therefore the Israelite is sinning as it were against existence itself whenever he places another person in distress.

Characteristic of the earliest literature of Israel then is also a great interest, exceptional in this ancient world, for what we call "the phenomenon of man." This appears specifically from the masterpiece that is called "the history of the succession to the throne." It describes how from among David's children, Solomon at last becomes his successor, as the outcome of a series of human dramas which are described with great literary skill and equally great care.

This concern for man is still more explicit in the great

historical work that is customarily attributed to "the Jahwist." We have seen that Wellhausen recognized this work as the foundation of the Pentateuchal narrative. Instead of 850 B. C., many scholars of the present time place that work in the reign of Solomon (approximately 970-930B. C.), and thus before the disintegration of David's kingdom. Perhaps we may summarize as follows what this author wanted to hold before his reading public. "The great kingdom of David which you are now witnessing and in which so many nations are incorporated is not to be taken for granted and is not a culmination. I have brought together all sorts of ancient sagas from the time before the state came into being, in order to let you see how our God Jahweh earlier prepared this great kingdom. And this society of so many peoples in the kingdom of Jahweh is not an end-point. For his intention is ultimately to bring together in it all nations, and to cause them to share in the blessing which he bestowed upon Abraham. For what he is concerned with is mankind as a totality, the *adam*. I am now letting you see this in my pre-history. Jahweh created man and wanted him to be one family. But man refused to acknowledge his divine sovereignty. The result was the trampling under foot of fellowmen. Cain murdered his brother, and Lamech avenged himself seventy-seven-fold. The sad story of a humanity that no longer acknowledges its Lord ends in the drama of the tower of Babel: the humanity that is meant to be God's family is broken apart, fragmented into innumerable nations that no longer understand each other. You must see the calling of Abraham against this background, and therewith also your own task in the history of mankind."

During the following centuries we see the basic features of Israel's religion come to expression primarily in the preaching of the prophets. While people are born everywhere and at all times with what we call a particular sensitivity for the religious, in Israel such gifted men naturally became "prophets," themselves called, and calling others. For their experience of the divine could not be anything but an experience of Jahweh, at least when they grew up in a milieu in which the old tradition was alive. Then this experience naturally acquired the character of a "calling." For people acknowledged Jahweh as a summons to followship, "covenant"; all the stories, rites, and agencies of the tradition stood under the sign of that covenant. Hence it is that through the very fact that they were seized by a strong sense of his presence, the prophets were aware of being "sent" to their people, to restore fellowship according to the original design: fellowship between Israel and Jahweh, and fellowship among men. Hence it is also that the prophetic preaching which is handed down to us is dominated by the two great themes of the Ten Commandments. It protests against the recognition of other powers than Jahweh, or against "idolatry," any tendency or effort to anticipate any salvation from any earthly or celestial agency. It also protests, in the name of this same Jahweh, against every form of injustice and oppression. Of course the emphasis varies with each prophet, depending on his temperament and the situation with which he had to deal. Let me give a couple of examples.

Around 840 B. C. we see Elijah, in the northern kingdom, taking a stand for the rights of God and man. He represents circles in which the Jahwistic faith was experienced in its original purity. In agricultural Israel people had begun to believe that rain and fertility must come from the local Baal, just as the Canaanite population had always thought. The king joined them zealously in this persuasion. Because of trading connections, King Ahab also had taken a princess from the Canaanite city of Tyre as his wife, and of course her Baal also got its own temple. According to Elijah, Israel was "limping", by acknowledging other powers alongside Jahweh. He fought furiously for the exclusive rights of Jahweh. Therefore he also took a firm stand against Ahab and his wife when she violated the property rights and took the life of an Israelite, Naboth, whom she had murdered in order to be able to add his vineyard to her own land.

While we know Elijah and his successor Elisha only from the splendidly related and so clearly proclamatory narratives about them, a number of utterances from one of their colleagues in the following century, Hosea, are handed down to us. Around 750 B. C. this Hosea had to deal with an Israel that thought it must give thanks for the produce of the land, grain and flax, oil and wine, to the local Baals, the "lovers" of Israel, thought of as a woman. In so doing, according to Hosea, Israel committed an offense against the love of Jahweh, her first and only Baal, that is, her husband and lord. Now he must cause disasters to come upon her, lay her land waste, in order once again to bring her, in this wilderness situation, back to her first love. Hosea thus illustrates the nature of the one who on his own initiative delivered people from Egypt, in order to make of them his own people, devoted to him alone. Especially famous are Hosea's sublime words about Jahweh as a passionate and jealous lover, and as a father who cannot give up his ungrateful and rebellious son, because his love is a divine love, and in measure, though not in kind, it transcends the human expressions of it. Israel now should respond to it with what Hosea calls "knowledge of God." Whenever this is lacking in the land, the land then is dominated by all that is destructive to human society: "Cursing, lying, murder, stealing, and adultery, and one bloody deed follows another." Hence his passionate reproach of the political and religious leaders who allow and perpetuate all this wickedness.

Some utterances from Hosea's contemporary Amos also have been handed down to us. He apparently lived in a village in the kingdom of Judah, in the ancient traditions of Jahwism. From there he traveled to the northern kingdom that had appropriated the ancient hallowed name of Israel. But that kingdom did not at all live up to the name. For Amos had heard that in this prosperous nation people were being exploited and trampled under foot. This cannot be reconciled with the name Israel. He went directly to the source of all that evil, the royal temple where the king and the priests met. There people reveled in believing perspectives on history and celebrated the faithfulness of Jahweh and his promises which are not repented of; he will give still more blessings, more prosperity, still clearer signs of his favoritism toward Israel.

This is the target against which Amos directs his attack, with a fierceness that is constantly amazing to the reader of the Bible. Election by Jahweh, perhaps; but then this can only mean that Israel bears a greater responsibility than other nations, and shall be more severely punished for every form of injustice. Do the Israelites think that they are more than others? The black people of Africa are just as precious to Jahweh! The exodus from Egypt: that must be the point of difference. But has not Jahweh had a hand in all the migrations of peoples? "I have also led the Philistines out of Caphtor and the Arameans out of Kir." Thus Amos sees him as the God of all nations, and primarily as the universal protector of human rights. When these rights are injured among his own people, then he will destroy them, without pardon. Perhaps he will let something remain of the nation; perhaps, but it may very well be that this remnant will be like the ear of a sheep, a bit of proof that the shepherd shows to the owner of the flock to demonstrate that the animal was mangled by a wild beast.

Shortly after Amos' time the great Isaiah takes a stand for the rights of God and man. It appears that those who compiled his book wanted to keep the reader in suspense. First of all, the reader hears, through several chapters, complaints and threats against the rulers and the people of Judah, who are boldly labeled, in the style of Amos, as princes of Sodom and people of Gomorrah. Isaiah could not have thought of any terms that would have been more offensive in that setting. All sorts of injustice were being practiced there at that time. Rich men were seizing the houses and fields of the poor, in order themselves to become the only property-holders in the country. Jahweh therefore loathes their religious observances in the temple, with sacrifices, praise, and incense. As it happened earlier in Egypt, now the cries of anguish of oppressed people will move him to intervene, to strike now for his people. The destroying armies of Assyria are already on the march.

At this point, in chapter 6, the compilers let Isaiah himself tell of his call. While the king of Assyria is preparing to become the only ruler in the entire world, in the year that the king from David's house in Jerusalem died, Isaiah sees *the* king, Jahweh of hosts, on his heavenly throne. The significance of this vision is appropriately described by Father Renckens. After he has dealt with the new import which the expression "Jahweh of hosts" has acquired, as world-God and creator-God, he writes:

"That worldwide character is shown to Isaiah in this vision. Hence this vision, put in positive terms, says: Jahweh is the God of the world and is beginning to reveal himself as God of the world; that is, what he was for Israel alone up to this time he shall be, in the future, for the entire world and for all mankind. Stated in negative terms: the time of Israel's national privileged position is past, Israel has had its chance and did not use it, Jahweh is turning from Israel and will undertake on a worldwide scale what he has not succeeded in achieving in Israel.

Isaiah encounters the ancient Jahweh of hosts, but now he is the God of the universe; the ancient Adonai, the national Master, but now the Lord Almighty; in Jerusalem's temple, but this place has cosmic dimensions; seated upon the ancient throne of the ark, but this has become the heavenly throne; the ancient Holy One of Israel, but now the thrice-holy God of the world, whose holiness is revealed in Israel in the cloud of glory, but whose glory now fills the whole earth; the ancient cherubim with their limited task of bearing the throne and guarding the gates appear, with Isaiah, ennobled and spiritualized into seraphim. The ultimate aim of all God's work is the revelation of his holiness. Jahweh's name must be hallowed on earth as it is in heaven, in order that the earth also may be full of his glory. From all eternity that ultimate aim in all its completeness is in God's view; that ultimate aim is the inexhaustible subject of the celestial liturgy. For one moment Isaiah is the privileged witness of it.

So much the more painfully then is he aware of the fact that he stands as a man in the middle of history, which as yet is only in the process of development toward that goal. The earth is still far from being full of Jahweh's glory, and the very nation in whose midst the King of glory dwells from of old is a sinful nation, a Sodom-people. It is his own people.

Thus this vision brings about a great change in Isaiah's mind: the salvation of Jahweh shall be for a new worldwide Israel; this salvation shall have, as its obverse side, great calamity for the old national Israel. When Isaiah then nevertheless begins to speak to a nation which is hopelessly lost, this is because it is brought home to him that a person of good will can be cleansed, even though it be by fire. The national catastrophe will be the purification and the salvation of many. Therefore Jahweh speaks through Isaiah in order, by means of his creative word, to form within his rejected nation a remnant out of which, as from a holy seed, the new Israel can grow."

This remnant will consist of people who believe, in the sense which Isaiah gives to this concept. They rely on Jahweh alone, and therefore they form a community which has as its motto "Immanuel," "God is with us." That is also the name of the one who represents this group, the one who will take the place of the unbelieving king Ahaz. Isaiah gives him grandiose names, but he does not call him king. That title belongs to Jahweh alone. Full of the Spirit of Jahweh, this ruler will bring justice to the poor and the oppressed, and his word alone will be fatal to the evildoers and the tyrants.

Thus Isaiah gives the first sketch of the future figure who later will be identified by the set term "Messiah." This picture is very closely related to his encounter with God and the proclamation to which he is driven on the basis of that encounter. Isaiah properly is often called the prophet of faith. Thanks to the many words which his disciples recorded, we see clearly in him what Renckens writes elsewhere, "that the prophets who must preach the collapse of the national framework are compelled to issue a call to a personal decision of faith and they begin to lay emphasis upon personal responsibility." He goes on to point out that they had to be the first to detach themselves from secure concealment in the collective body. "Thus the collapse of the national framework drives people to what is personal and inward, while this in turn opens their eyes to the inadequacy of the national framework."

Jeremiah was present for this collapse. In the biblical book that preserves so many of his utterances, we hear the two classical themes repeatedly sounded: protest against idolatry and protest against social injustice. They are combined in his famous indictment of temple worship which almost cost him his life. "Steal, murder, commit adultery, swear falsely, run after Baals, — and then come and worship Jahweh in the temple and imagine that you are safe there!" Therefore this temple will be destroyed.

This prophet appears not to think in worldwide terms. It is in keeping with his character that he seeks the universal, as it were, in the depths. He touches upon it where he describes the workings of "the heart," what is deepest within man, from which issues all that he thinks and does. There is no grand portrayal of the Messiah in his book, but there is the anticipation of an entirely new relation between Jahweh and his people, one which is no longer dependent upon external structures because it is rooted in the hearts of men.

The universal nature of belief in Jahweh is very impressively expressed during the exile by the prophet who speaks in Isaiah 40-55. The topic of social injustice no longer needs to be treated; the old social structures no longer exist, and the deportation to Babylon has brought all the Judeans into the selfsame condition. The prophet is speaking to people who in spite of everything are striving to believe that Jahweh has not broken the relation with his people and intends to make a new beginning. The prophet wants to strengthen this belief, and he does this by means of his proclamation of a new exodus, a definitive version of the first exodus out of Egypt. For this will result in a grand restoration of Zion. This saving and delivering appearance, in which Jahweh will bring to life again his defunct people, will convincingly show the whole world the true nature of Jahweh. "All flesh," that is, all mankind, will behold his salvation, and to the very ends of the earth every knee will bow before him.

Here the concern for mankind on the part of Israel's God is eloquently expressed. Yet a still further development will be necessary in order to come to the situation in which Jesus will bring the ancient faith to a full unfolding.

3. The crisis of separatism

We have already met Ezra as "the father of Judaism." Without his zeal the Jewish community would have been overwhelmed by influences from without and ultimately would have been swallowed up in "the melting-pot of Hellenism." Then no Jesus of Nazareth, and no Bible, would have been possible. Hence a look at this period is important for the reader of the Bible. Therefore some comments are in order, first about the emphasizing of separatism by the book of Deuteronomy.

This book of law belongs to the national revival in Judah in the time of king Josiah (approximately 640-609 B. C.). A century earlier, powerful Israel had been destroyed by the Assyrians, an evident punishment by Jahweh of that alliance with the Baals of the country. If Judah would have a future, then every trace of this pagan religion must be rooted out, and everyone who took part in it or encouraged it must be pitilessly removed from the national community. The book of law urged total loyalty and love toward Jahweh, with the whole soul and with all one's powers, and a pure worship of Him alone in *one* place. This has reference to the temple in Jerusalem, but because the book of law is attributed to Moses, this city could not be identified by name.

Connected with this turning to Jahweh is the fact that the book of law gives a great deal of attention to the welfare of one's fellowmen, particularly of the dispossessed, such as the poor, widows, orphans, and foreigners; it even urges kind treatment of animals. But to render secure this loyalty to Jahweh, it also prescribes the strictest regulations against those who are guilty of worshiping other gods or who lead others to do so. The fiction that it is Moses who gives these laws means that Israel is regarded as not yet having arrived in Canaan. Hence the command to place the anathema, as it is called, upon all the cities of that land, that is, to root out all the inhabitants; "otherwise they will lead you to participate in all the abominable things that they have practiced for their gods."

In this spirit, under king Josiah, the great national epic was assembled which in our Bible is given in the books beginning with Joshua and going through Kings. The most strongly "idealized" part is the conduct of Joshua. He is supposed to have done, in the conquest, what Moses had prescribed, and to have killed all the inhabitants of the conquered cities. It is good to know that in reality this did not happen thus, and that it is fictional, "preaching in narrative form."

The influence of Deuteronomy is clearly seen in the rules which are described in Ezra 9 and 10: all the women of non-Jewish origin, together with their children, are expelled from the community. Yet it would be incorrect to portray the further development of the Jewish life of faith as an intensifying experience of this religious separatism. For other ideas also were alive: other texts, with a more inclusive view, were read, such as stories by the Jahwist and the words of Deutero-Isaiah, while other new ones were added. Job and his friends, to whom Jahweh addressed himself personally, are pagans; they do not belong to Israel. In Proverbs 8, Wisdom, represented as a woman, is concerned, from the creation onward, with the felicity in life of all mankind.

The pretty little story about Ruth could be intended as a protest against the regulations of Ezra. The heroine is a Moabite woman, a member of a nation from which no one might ever be admitted to Jahweh's community. The writer pictures her as a very noble woman, and has her become an ancestress of no less a figure than king David. The splendid brief narrative about Jonah also appears to have been written as a sharp condemnation of the dominant mentality. The pagan members of the ship's crew are appealing and God-fearing, and the inhabitants of Nineveh promptly do what the Israelites never have done: they all sincerely repent as soon as a prophet summons them to do so. The only repelling figure in the story is Jonah, a symbol of narrowness of sympathy and self-interest which have become characteristic of the Jewish community. He tries to escape from his commission to proclaim salvation to the heathen and he becomes enraged when Jahweh does not destroy these heathen. The capable writer of this narrative reaches a climactic point when he has the prophet express his exasperation in one of the most splendid formulations of Israel's faith: "I knew it! I knew that you are a gracious God, merciful, longsuffering, and abundant in pity!" But the very idea of a God who cares for people outside his own nation is for Jonah so intolerable that he asks to be allowed to die. A sharper criticism of the Jewish separatism can hardly be conceived.

Still other Jews chose the prophetic style to give expression to their belief in the worldwide saving intentions of their God. Thus there is the familiar vision of the temple-mountain, to which, at the end of time, all nations will ascend in order to learn from Jahweh how they must live with each other; then they shall re-shape all their weaponry into instruments of prosperity and peace. It is highly significant that this enraptured description was incorporated into two collections of prophetic sayings, Isaiah 2 and Micah 4. A text of universal intent was added also to earlier utterances in Isaiah 19: Egypt and Assyria, those archenemies of earlier times, will turn in a fraternal spirit to Jahweh, and Israel will participate as a third member in this covenant, a blessing in the midst of the earth. There is something almost biting in the fact that expressions which in the language of the covenant and election are used for Israel as God's own people are applied here to the two great oppressors of earlier times: "Jahweh shall say, 'Blessed Egypt, *my people*; Assyrians, *the work of my hands*; Israel, *my inheritance!*'"

By way of supplementing these data from the Bible itself, I should like to refer here to what Renckens wrote about the great significance of the period after Ezra, the Jewish period in biblical history. It is understandable, he says, that we feel sympathy for the warm and human figures of the prophets and their deep and universalist views. We have little feeling for a religious experience that gave the Law such a central position and that appears to us as a wicked rigidity. Therefore it is good to remember that in these centuries it was the believers who brought the Old Testament into being, the Hebrew form of it as well as the Greek translation. That Judaism is to be regarded as the first actualization of "the remnant" which the prophets had proclaimed, and with which Jahweh would continue after the destruction of the national structures. In their view this remnant would consist of humble men, a "poor" people, not only poor in material things, but primarily in the religious sense that they not only had lost their earthly goods and aids, but also could no longer put any trust in such. They would seek their refuge in Jahweh alone. Let me quote Renckens again:

"In his day-by-day faithfulness to the law the Jew experiences his poverty, that is, his total surrender to his God. Far from securing for himself a human guarantee of salvation through strict fulfillment of the law, by that very obedience he confesses that God himself is his only stay. For him the Law is everything, because for him it is the summation of God's way to man and thus also the only way of man to his God. Thus minor prescriptions become important and they can be fulfilled with a ready heart. When the Jew glories in the Law of Jahweh, this is a glorying of faith. The national collapse which deprived the Jew of every human support and literally made him poor became, through faith, an experience with God; what had been a national disaster was understood, in faith, as a gracious judgment of God who in his very withdrawal maintains a remnant of believers and comes to them."

Thus the Jewish writings in the Bible, that is, the books which came into existence in the Jewish period, and those which are preserved only in the Septuagint, must not be read in the nationalistic and legalistic spirit in which they were later understood, but in terms of the spirit in which they arose.

Renckens characterizes this later spirit thus: "The official Judaism of the time of Christ had forgotten the spirit out of which it was born and gradually had come to seek, in all sorts of externals and in racism, an all-too-human guarantee of salvation." We have tried to comprehend this attitude in the perspective of the struggle and the sacrifices of the Maccabeans. It is evident that from that time people thought in completely negative terms about the other nations, then united into the Hellenistic world. This world appeared to the loyal Jews as the most avowed enemy of their community, God's only domain on this earth. Of the four beasts which Daniel sees rising out of the sea, the last one is the most dreadful.

In Jesus' day, then, the view was predominant that there was no hope at all for the other nations. Only the faithful fulfilling of the Law could give any prospect for a future with God. That was the official teaching. Yet not all the rabbis were entirely comfortable with this view. The English biblical scholar W. D. Davies speaks in this connection of an "uneasy conscience." He sees an indication of this in the diverse opinions about the proselytes. There were Jews who, as Jesus says in Matthew's account, "cross sea and land in order to make a single convert." They believed that a Gentile had a chance to survive only if he was incorporated as fully as possible into the chosen people and, as it were, took on the Jewish nationality. According to a rabbi from the beginning of the second century, God had scattered the Jews among the nations with precisely that aim, that they might make as many proselytes as possible. However, that was not the opinion of all the rabbis, and the attitude of some with respect to the proselytes was, to say the least, equivocal. In any case, it is not true that in Jesus' time the heathen were regarded simply as written off, so completely so that there was no need any longer even to talk about them.

For they were discussed. This is evident from the theories which were propounded to prove that the other nations had been given the same chances as had Israel. It was through their own fault that they had come into this hopeless condition. One of these theses stated that at one time God had offered the Law at Sinai to all nations. Only Israel had accepted this gift; all others had rejected the offer and thus had forfeited their only chance of salvation.

Alongside this there arose also the theory that God had sent prophets to the Gentiles. Taking the figure of Balaam in the book of Numbers as a starting point, some related that he was sent as a prophet to the Gentiles just as Moses was sent to Israel. He grew to be seven prophets, all of whom were rejected by the heathen nations.

Thus when Jesus appeared in the Jewish community, that community was familiar with something like a "Gentile problem." And there is every reason to believe that this was the real problem with which the zealous Pharisee who in his Jewish environment was named Saul was wrestling.

Because the conviction of Jewish separatism was much

more deeply rooted in him than in the Galileans whom Jesus had gathered around himself as a "core-group," Paul also was much more keenly sensitive than they to the manner in which Jesus had abolished this separatism by allowing all men without distinction to share in Israel's privilege. Therefore Paul's later life was consumed in a worldwide activity, in order to create everywhere those radiating centers of the universal "family of God" that Jesus had had in view.

Referring back to the sketch of Jesus' conduct in our first chapter, we can summarize what has been said here as follows. At the root of Israel's religion lay an experience of the divine as "person," as appeal to and offer of fellowship. In the centuries after the exile, the tension increased between this universalist datum and the concern to stand apart in the experience of this "given." Jesus appeared at the climactic point of this tension. He lived through it, all the way to death. Thus he was experienced as the embodiment of the appeal that is called "God," and hence as the very center of a universal human community.

4. Inspiration for "a new confessionalism"

"It all sounds too modern for me, and especially too humanistic. In this entire approach to Israel's religion and to Jesus' intentions is there not a great lot of mosaic work, patchwork, being practiced?" Objections along this line undoubtedly will be raised. My answer would be that of course some "mosaic work" has been practiced. No one can view the past other than through his own eyes, or, better said, through the spectacles of his own time, which he cannot take off. I am conscious also of what a biblical scholar — an Anglo-Saxon, of course — identified in a book title as "the peril of modernizing Jesus." But as my real answer I want to point to the fact that the first generations of believers accepted and experienced Christianity in just this way: as a belief that founded a fellowship. This was recently emphasized again by students of the Greco-Roman world who are studying the rapid spread of Christianity. The Dominican Festugiere, a great expert on the many religious tendencies in that world, in 1961 concluded a brief study of the ancient Greek folk-religion with this personal comment: "If I should be permitted to set forth to you my own feelings, the feelings of a dyed-in-the-wool historian who has reflected endlessly on the mysterious transition from Greek paganism to the Christian faith, I would say this: what brought these pagans to conversion was not so much the novelties in the doctrine which was proclaimed to them. as it was the example of mutual love that the Christians gave, and the impression that the converts gained when they joined the Christians' fellowship. At last someone loved them, at last they were no longer alone.... This was what was totally new about Christianity. This touched the hearts; this brought about conversion. Not the word, but the example. Or, better said, the truth of the word as demonstrated by the example. The sublimities of the doctrine usually went over people's heads, just as they do today. But the unwearying love for neighbors, this they saw, and in this they shared."

The English student E. Dodds agrees with this view. The spectacles which he wears are somewhat different from those of Festugiere. In his masterful study of the relationship between pagans and Christians in this earliest period, he says that he has no religious convictions at all. His book then is also one of surprising soberness. When at the conclusion of the book he discusses some of the psychological advantages which furthered the growth of the Christian faith and contributed to its victory, he names as the last and most prominent one the influence of the Christian life of fellowship.

"Modern social studies have brought home to us the universality of the "need to belong" and the unexpected ways in which it can influence human behaviour, particularly among the rootless inhabitants of great cities. I see no reason to think that it was otherwise in antiquity: Epictetus has described for us the dreadful loneliness that can beset a man in the midst of his fellows. Such loneliness must have been felt by millions — the urbanised tribesman, the peasant come to town in search of work, the demobilised soldier, the rentier ruined by inflation, and the manumitted slave. For people in that situation membership of a Christian community might be the only way of maintaining their self-respect and giving their life some semblance of meaning. Within the community there was human warmth: some one was interested in them, both here and hereafter. It is therefore not surprising that the earliest and the most striking advances of Christianity were made in the great cities — in Antioch, in Rome, in Alexandria. Christians were in a more than formal sense "members one of another": I think that was a major cause, perhaps the strongest single cause, of the spread of Christianity."

Thus our description of what Jesus actually had in mind is no modern, humanistic interpretation. It is true that these experts on early Christianity make it clear to us that the *conceptions* of the faith in this first period were different from what they can be now among us. A clear view of this fact appears to me to be *of capital importance* for our ecumenical efforts.

We have seen that the gospels give us a portrait of Jesus which is also a particular interpretation. There he is understood and portrayed in a biblical manner, "biblicized," and this in a way which could speak to people in the Greco-Roman world. This way has become foreign to us. To take one example, it was not the human attributes of Jesus which impressed them when the gospel was proclaimed to them. In their eyes he was first of all the son of God manifest among men, announced in advance through prophecy, performing numerous wonders, and after his death ascended into glory. Another expert on early Christianity, A. D. Nock, writes that for them Jesus "is a powerful savior rather than a model; the Christian manner of life is something that is made possible by Christ the Lord in the midst of his community, rather than something that issues out of their following after him. In the center stands the idea of the deity who has come among men in order to fulfill the plan of salvation, and not that of a perfected man who has come in order to inspire us.... The magnetism of Jesus' personality had played a part in the gathering of his first disciples, although even then the impression of power probably was more important than that of love; in later times the only human qualities which had influence were those of individual Christian leaders and disciples."

Thus for Nock also it is the human qualities of Christians which exert this drawing power, not those of Jesus himself. He was esteemed primarily for his God-likeness. Profound utterances concerning this character no doubt will "go right over the heads" of many people, as Festugiere assumed. It is already said in the New Testament itself that difficult passages appear in Paul's epistles. All this affects the interpretation of Jesus' person and work.

Now it seems to me that a line runs from this point to the separated Christian churches, each with its own "confession." When the persecutions were past and the Christian movement was frozen into an officially recognized religion, people had time and opportunity to bring together the conceptions of the New Testament, that is, still uncoordinated interpretations of Jesus, and to fix them in thought-out dogmatic formulations, dogmas. This is rather broadly stated, I know. But still I venture to ask whether the later separation of the Christian churches does not go back in part to divergent, contrasting elaborations of these dogmas.

If this is correctly seen, then an honestly thought-through historical approach to the Bible should contribute strength to the ecumenical striving of the churches, perhaps even more than it has already done. It can set forth the real intentions of Jesus, and can do this in such a way that they can be translated into elementary wording. Therewith it relativizes the dogmatic formulations which by their very nature have a divisive effect. Then the churches will be able to gather all their energies to give heed to a summons which for Christians is a divine summons, heard in the need of their fellowmen. In our time that is the need of an entire humanity which is threatened with destruction. Faith in Jesus urges collaboration with all others who, regardless of who or where they may be, are doing something that will further the common life of people and will give perspective to it. In his own distinctive terse style, F. Tellegen recently wrote about *the new type of confessionalism* that is now in the making. According to him "it must be designed in such a way that believers and non-believers, as well as those of differing beliefs, can in reason see the effect of it and experience it as a contribution to the solution of the vital questions of all people." Through this new form of confessionalism the message of salvation can enter into present-day history and become effective in it, when two conditions are fulfilled. The first of these is that the claim of Christians to possess the only true faith is relativized, in word and in fact, and further that this confessionalism will give priority to human cooperation, to current vital issues and hence to working together on them; thus Tellegen.

Further, this new form of confessionalism must be dynamic and flexible, and must not reserve for itself and maintain any terrain of activity or its own setting. "Activity with reference to the current vital issues belongs in principle to all men, to all collaboration, teamwork. Christians, as messengers of salvation, have no authority at all to infringe upon this right. They, just the same as all other men, must seek for what there is for us, human beings, to do here and now. But they should be conscious of the question of how the message of salvation can have meaning, through Christians, in this collaboration, of how they can function in it." They must strive anew to determine this in every new situation. There are no rules for it. "The new confessionalism will have to be a manifest service to all mankind. It must be carried by inspired and inspiring Christians, just as flexible as the changed world itself is."

In this view, Christians have no contribution of their own to make as far as *content* is concerned, when they work together with others in service to mankind. The only thing that is unique therein is their motivation or inspiration. For them this lies in the person whose name they bear, Christ, one of the titles of the man from Nazareth who was named Jesus.

Precisely in connection with his person as the source of inspiration, it seems to me extremely important that we have clearly in mind what he, as man among us men, has done, and by what motives he himself was inspired. He wanted to give expression in his life to what has been identified in our sketch as the fellowship-founding character of God. He took up the cause of those who were expelled from this community of God, the "sinners." He steadfastly persisted in this attitude, in that making visible and tangible God's disposition, even when he knew that his life itself would be consumed therein. Just before his death he expressed this during his last meal with his disciples. In his gesture with bread and wine he summed up what inspired him, what meaning he gave to the death that would consummate his human life and through which, so to speak, he would begin to belong to the past, or would pass into history. By means of this gesture of self-giving in the form of bread and wine he created the possibility of continuing to be active in this history precisely in what constituted his life, the summons to be a community.

We must remember that after his death his disciples did not acquire any new historical data about him. In the mysterious experiences thereafter the assurance was granted to them that in him God continued to address himself to men. The faith so deeply permeated their lives, and had such powerful effects, that they saw the Spirit of God at work therein. The picturing and formulating of all that they had gone through with

Jesus also fell under this impact. It was interpretation, translation, explanation of that bit of history that was once and for all concluded. The writer of the fourth gospel appears to have indicated by Christ himself what the Holy Spirit would do after his departure: he would bring to the disciples' remembrance what Jesus had said to them and he would cause them to understand what his mission, his life, and his death signify for men.

As was said earlier, the interpretations offered by later Christian doctrine arose out of the interpretations which the New Testament has preserved. There arose a doctrine about the three Persons in God, the incarnation, redemption, the sacraments, the church, and much else besides. Not only did the diverse elaborations of doctrine play a role in the succeeding centuries in the splintering of Christian communities which began to arise alongside and in opposition to each other and thereby obscured the message which they claimed to embody. But these elaborated doctrinal theses and formulas also came to have less and less content for people of the new era. The preaching in the churches now no longer has any connection for a great many Christians with the world of their experience.

Therefore it appears to me of vital importance for the proclamation to refer back to that closed bit of history with which the first disciples after Jesus' death also had to deal. For that has to do with actual men who encountered each other, experienced all sorts of relationships, and came into conflict with each other. Everyone, regardless of time and place, who lives his life in company with others can sense what all this means.

Most Christians, however, cannot have a feeling for a number of the interpretations. That Jesus on the cross paid the price for our sins once and for all, and that he then wrought our redemption by means of the price of his blood, — these are conceptions which for some of the writers of the New Testament were expressive statements of what Jesus meant, in their view, for mankind. Perhaps the more detailed and elaborate theories of redemption in later centuries were also expressive for the men of that time. But in the present time many Christians are saying quite honestly, "What does it mean now that I am redeemed on the cross? What do I see of that now?"

In the first centuries of the church the believers did discern what was meant by redemption. They came into a milieu that was characterized by, or at least strove for, mutual respect and love, and unwearying service. Hence Jesus appeared to be working redemptively. In his spirit something was realized there of the common life as "God's family" that he had had in mind. In our time, believers, non-believers, and those of a different belief will have to be able to "see and experience" the effect of our confession "as a contribution to the solution of vital questions of all people," as Tellegen has formulated it. And it seems to me that the inspiration to this achievement can constantly be fed by the preaching of Jesus, and the encounter with Jesus, as he actually lived among us men and is summed up in his service.

5. No biblical proof of faith

What now can the function of the Bible be, in this new form of confessionalism? Here emerges the extremely difficult question as to the "authority" of that book. Previously, for this authority reference was made, among other things, to the miraculous history which was related by the Bible with a divine guarantee. It appears to be useful to go into this matter briefly here.

The "old" confessions were characterized by the concern for the pure formulation of the truth of faith. Sometimes the impression was aroused that this truth could be proved. This certainly was the case in Roman Catholic circles. In the nineteen-thirties I received, in secondary school, religious instruction from an "apologetics book," a defense of the Catholic faith in three divisions. During my theological training these books were replaced by hefty manuals in Latin, which provided still more detailed proofs. We began with the existence of God. Then there followed the proof that he can reveal, then that in fact he has done so, and so it went all the way to and including the proof that the church of Rome is the only true church of Christ. I do not know how the matter went in Protestant circles. I have been assured, however, that in orthodox churches of Calvinistic flavor proofs of this apologetic kind were customary also. When we earlier discussed, in our second chapter, the reactions from the orthodox side to the historical approach, we saw, in fact, points of agreement between the ways in which it was rejected by the teaching authority of Rome and by Protestant defenders of the old belief.

An important link in the above-mentioned proof was formed by the miracles and the fulfilled prophecies which the Bible relates. A miracle was defined as an event which cannot be wrought by any natural forces. Sometimes the definition read: a miracle is an interruption of the regularities which are inherent in nature; now only God can break these laws which he himself has established; when a man performs such a miracle, he can do this only in the power of God, and then all that he affirms must also be covered by God's authority. Knowledge of the future also is reserved to God alone. If something happens that was announced far in advance by someone, proof is provided therewith that this person had received his foreknowledge directly from God.

Nowadays these proofs no longer suffice. They are now regarded as irrelevant, invalid, and even misleading. Of the many factors which have led to this development, I wish to mention only three.

First of all, the idea that *faith and proof are mutually exclusive*. Believing lies on a different plane from that of insights and certainties which can be proven. Believing lies on the plane of personal relationships. Love between two persons is based upon choice and upon surrender; these lie outside the realm of proofs. In a good marriage the spouses have no need of proofs of mutual love. Expressions of it are indeed called for, but these presuppose faith in each other on the part of the spouses. As soon as there is something amiss in that faith, no expression by the one can serve as proof for the other that he or she really is loved. Even the most expensive gift cannot restore the relationship. It can be interpreted by the other person who no longer has faith as a "maneuver," whatever the intention may be. So long as this other person does not surrender, he or she cannot be convinced by any gesture.

Since the prophet Hosea it cannot be called irreverent to describe biblical faith in terms of human love, not even in the intensified form of love which we call "being in love." In giving instruction in the faith I like to point to three elements in love by which the faith of Israel can be explained. Love comes upon a person, it gives him a new view of everything, both of the beloved one and of the world, and he is unable to express all this in suitable words, let alone prove it.

Thus Israel bears witness that it has been *seized* by this special relationship with God. The initiative always proceeds from him. Abraham suddenly hears the voice calling him. And he appears in Moses' life when Moses is unsuspectingly keeping his sheep near a thicket. And thus it is again and again in the further history. Thereby Israel gained a *view of God* such as no other people had. They saw him as an omnipotent power, gracious and merciful. They saw him at work in creation, in history, and in all that happens. When other men said that the Assyrians were making plans to undertake a campaign against Syria and Palestine, believing Israelites said that it was their God who had summoned their armies to Palestine. For outsiders this was *incomprehensible language*. All that was said of their God Jahweh by prophets and lawgivers and leaders, about his commands and his world-encompassing promises, and all that they confessed together in their songs of praise and prayers, — all this was hardly understandable to others. To someone who stood outside this community of faith, no Israelite could prove that his experience concerned the deepest reality and was the loftiest truth.

Then it is my custom to show how these elements also can be seen in the faith of Jesus' first disciples, and in that of the later church. When an abundance of expressions of the faith becomes the possession of a large group in a religion that gains general acceptance down through the centuries, these can grow then into a system of truths which are identified as "revealed," but it is easily forgotten that they stem from the language of love, and that they are both inadequate and unprovable.

As a second factor I should like to name the increasing conviction *that for every phenomenon in this world there must be an explanation,* and connected with this, the anticipation that the explanation will sometime be found. It is true that the natural scientists now think otherwise than did their colleagues of the last century about the possibilities of their specialty; still there remains the fact that this conviction has become an accepted assumption among men in our western world, and for them miracle stories cannot be proof of an intervention by God.

The third factor is *the historical study of the Bible.* This study showed that stories about marvelous events and about predictions which came true were not intended as factual reporting. They appeared to belong to the forms in which biblical men gave expression to their faith, to be able to express that faith together, to "celebrate," and to be able to hand it on to succeeding generations. Because it is important for readers of the Bible in our time to see this clearly, I shall go into this matter briefly.

A little earlier I referred to the military campaigns of the Assyrians. I find in them a clear illustration of the point I am making here. We know a great deal about the Assyrian culture and history in the time of Isaiah. Even though there are gaps in our knowledge about the campaigns which Tiglath-Pileser and his successors undertook to "the west," in themselves these were purely mundane events. The reasons why the Assyrian king undertook them, the organization of them, and the results issuing from them — all this was in principle knowable. No doubt the diplomats in Jerusalem were quite well informed on the matter. Yet Isaiah says that it is Jahweh who has brought the Assyrians into action. He has "given them the signal" to march to Judah and to destroy that land.

Isaiah sees the visible and intrinsically understandable event as a gesture, an action, of Jahweh. What comes upon Israel is a part of its interrelationship with God. God addresses himself to his people through events, and his spokesman, the prophet, discloses the personal meaning of these events.

A biblical narrative about this could have run as follows: "The king of Assyria lay fast asleep. Suddenly his room was filled with a heavenly light. There appeared to him an angel of the Lord who awakened him and said, 'O king, gather your army and march to the land of Judah and its capital city Jerusalem. For thus says the Lord: I have seen the sins of my people and I am sending you to punish them....'"

Incidentally, this story does not appear in the Bible. But there are many others which have the same background: a belief that sees God at work in particular events, and expresses this by telling about an angel whom he has sent, a phenomenon in nature that he causes to happen, or in some other way. When we spoke of the Chronicler we noted how he introduced new miracles into an old story in order to make the story more clearly say what he believed. The ten plagues which, according to the book of Exodus, afflicted Egypt are the result of a combining of earlier plague-narratives. From an analysis of Exodus 14 it appears that the earliest kernel of this text did not describe the passage through the Red Sea as a miracle. An east wind blew, and pushed the shallow water back so that the fleeing Semitic slaves were able to escape their pursuers. The latter were stuck in the morass and were drowned when the wind changed. An Egyptian who escaped drowning could have said, "That bunch had a bit of good luck, and we had bad luck" (we may note parenthetically that this is not likely, for Egyptians were believers too; they too saw the hand of their gods in events of any importance.). In the light of Moses' faith the event took on significance as a revelation of God's saving nature. To put it in the words of H. Berkhof, the passage through the water "is usually presented as the central revelational event on which the faith of Israel has lived through the centuries. This is not incorrect, so long as we see that *this event in itself did not have a revelational character, but it acquired this through the context in which it was experienced.*"

These examples may suffice. Only the following may be emphasized. In antiquity, a phenomenon that was noteworthy, striking, or that had an impact upon life could more readily be seen as an act of God than we modern men can imagine. People did not seek at once for a natural explanation. The need for an understandable explanation was not as strong, and the concept of nature as a system of forces governed by laws was unknown.

We must keep this in mind particularly in connection with the miracles in the gospels. Anyone who takes a properly historical approach to them will avoid the customary term and will speak instead of the miracle-*stories* of the gospels. Upon analysis a great variety emerges. Only a few of them are entirely or partially "symbolic." We may think of the changing of water into wine at Cana and the raising of Lazarus, both in the fourth gospel. In other miracle-stories the significance of what is told obviously has had an influence on the literary form. I have in mind what we earlier heard Origen discuss: anyone who believes in Christ experiences his spiritual power which heals inward blindness, the leprosy of sin, and so forth. Yet the more careful analysis leads us to recollections of a life that was characterized by a number of miraculous healings. Imagine that some men of our time had been present there; then perhaps they could have given some explanation in what we call "psychosomatic" terms, that is, in terms of the influence which strong internal disturbances can have on the condition of the body and its organs. But it is not possible to transport modern men to that time, and besides, even then their "explanation" would not have been relevant. What Berkhof wrote about the revelational character that an event acquires "through the context in which it was experienced" applies here in a very special way. Anyone who met Jesus and opened himself to him realized something of a deeper dimension in what he said and did. He had indicated this once himself when he referred to the men of Nineveh in the story of Jonah and to the visit of the Oriental queen: "Behold, a greater than Jonah is here, a greater than Solomon is here." When Jesus expelled the evil spirits which tormented men, then people indeed sensed, according to the biblical expression attributed to Jesus himself, "the finger of God" at work. But once again, you had to be open to him if you wanted to discern this. Those who remained closed did recognize that he was doing superhuman things. But that, according to their insulting comment, came from "Beelzebub, the prince of devils." Others said that he had been under the instruction of Egyptian sorcerers.

Mark writes that Jesus could do no miracles in Nazareth because the people there did not believe in him. Later he notes that Jesus refused to accede to the Pharisees' demand that he give them "a sign from heaven" as proof of his mission. They were asking for something that was utterly impossible. Even the most expensive gift cannot have a convincing effect on a spouse who has lost his faith in his partner.

The story of a prediction that comes true can no more

function as proof than can the story of a miracle. Often it is clearly an expression of faith. David conquered the Edomites, a kindred nation that was established earlier than Israel. Believing that this subjection was in the plans of Jahweh, people had it announced in a word from God to the pregnant Rebekah concerning her sons Jacob (Israel) and Esau (Edom): the elder would be servant to the younger. Similarly Israel felt its living in the land of Canaan as a gift from Jahweh. They expressed this by having God promise it to the patriarchs. Where we are told of promises which God made to Abraham, Isaac, and Jacob, we are dealing with expressions of faith.

We find an actual prediction in Jeremiah 28. The prophet spoke this word from God to Hananiah: "Before the year is gone you will die." This happened, too. For Baruch, who wrote this down, it was undoubtedly a proof that Jeremiah was a true prophet. But his enemies could give a different explanation, for example, that Hananiah had already been looking so ill in recent times.

We described earlier the important role of the "messianic prophecies" in the proclamation of the young church. Here also it is evident that for us they can no longer serve as arguments. It is clear that there can be no proofs for our faith. Some believers are shocked by this and feel themselves robbed of their old certainties. Others prize the positive consequences; for example, this one.

The apologetic presentation of proof of earlier times was so thorough that it actually suggested that anyone who did not accept it and remained outside the Mother Church *must be of an evil will.* A younger sister of mine appeared to have digested the religious instruction at school quite well when she asked a visitor whether he was a Catholic. When he answered in the negative, she resolutely responded with "Then you are going to hell!" and then, "What a pity! you are such a nice man." We can laugh at this now. It was the spirit of a closed group, which reserved the truth and eternal salvation for its own members. At that time there were such groups in the Protestant world also. But in earlier centuries this mentality was, for many people, nothing to laugh at. When Christianity became the state religion, the official truth, and Christendom arose, life became unbearable for those who could not accept the official teaching. I am thinking in particular of the Jewish communities everywhere in Europe. The accepted view was that they had to be possessed of an evil will. Therefore it was permissible to rob them, persecute them, and torment them. Of course all sorts of factors of a social and economic nature quickly came to play a part. But the first and most prominent was their resistance to "the truth." An American rabbi who is studying Judaism and the modern currents in it recently wrote about the "revolutionary changes" which Judaism has experienced in the course of its history. As the first one he names the destruction of the state of Judah in 578 B. C. and the deportation to Babylon, and as the second the destruction of Jerusalem by the Romans in A. D. 70. The third revolutionary change which he names was "a result of the ideas which inspired the American and the French Revolutions. Long treated as an outcast in Christian society, the Jew, at last, was also to benefit from the recognition of the Rights of Man. The Ghetto walls fell. Emancipation came to the Jew in the West." This happened in the same time in which people began to approach the Bible historically. We have seen specifically how vigorously orthodox groups set themselves in opposition to this approach.

In conclusion, something about the divine character of the Bible. In my sketch of what Jesus preached and that for which he wholly committed himself, I have avoided the term "kingdom of God." I sincerely hope that the reader has not noticed this. For that would strengthen me in a conviction that has grown through the years. I think that with a great many people in our time the proclamation of the faith can reach its aim only when we *replace a number of traditional terms with others,* which are more comprehensible, and less heavily laden. It must be possible to transpose the intentions of Jesus into comprehensible language.

Now one of the expressions which, as I see it, must be avoided, at least temporarily, is this: *the Bible is the Word of God.* It evokes the idea that it is God who has written the Bible, and further, that God addresses himself directly to the person who reads the Bible or hears it read. This idea is not correct. With a great mass of complicated arguments theologians can indeed demonstrate that the expression can properly be understood. But for the ordinary believer it is misleading. For in the Bible only men are speaking.

Thanks to the historical approach we have discovered the immensely diverse expressions of men who stood in the same tradition of faith. The Old Testament bears witness to what life becomes in a group which goes through history with the belief in one God, in various social forms, first in a league of tribes, then as a kingdom (soon divided into two), and then in the unique form of Judaism, a form of society for which there is no parallel. Much of what went on among men in this believing tradition is reflected in the texts. Some of these texts are written from the perspective of a very intimate association with this one God, from the very core of the community, so to speak. Others are rather from the perspective of the structures within which this community moved. We may think of Jeremiah's conversations with God *alongside* the detailed prescriptions for worship in the book of Leviticus; or of the descriptions of the national heroes in Judges and Samuel *alongside* the wise counsels for a happy life in Proverbs; or of so many ardent prayers and hymns in the book of Psalms *alongside* the skeptical views of Ecclesiastes.

Those who speak in the Old Testament are all human, even when they say, "Thus says Jahweh...." Then they are expressing what they believe that God has to say to his people at that moment. Hence God speaks in Jeremiah in an entirely different style, with different images, and with a different choice of words from those in Isaiah.

Jesus also interpreted what God had to say to his people. But he never introduced his sayings with the formula, "Thus says Jahweh." *God's intentions and desires were so completely his own that he did not need to make this distinction.*

The men who speak in the New Testament speak from within the believing tradition which is based upon Jesus, from within the community which arose through the recognition of him as sole Lord. In various ways they bear witness to what happens in thought and life and society when all these come to be dominated by faith in Jesus.

The recognition of all this does not mean that one *thus* regards the Bible as an ordinary human book. Being a Christian consists in one's confessing Jesus as his Lord. One recognizes that in Jesus the God of Israel has expressed himself fully, that he is the climactic point of a believing tradition which is oriented to this God of Israel. In that tradition, alongside lawgivers and prophets, written words also play a role. Thus to the eye of faith, the books of the Old Testament share in this pre-history. The first church is included in the Jesus-event. There began the believing tradition in which we place ourselves when we accept Jesus as our Lord. The books of the New Testament constitute a part of this foundational stage of our fellowship. This is why they are for us so special and irreplaceable.

It seems to me that the conception of biblical authors such as Moses, Isaiah, and Matthew whom God inspired, into whom he breathed, or to whom he dictated what they must write, is incorrect and misleading. It is incorrect because several of the books actually were the work of many, nameless authors, and the deposit of a long tradition. It is misleading, because it easily isolates the Bible from that which for Christians possesses the highest authority, the claims and promises of Jesus. About this he left no obscurity. And it is Matthew, more of a scribe than the other evangelists, who has handed down to us the most impressive picture of the final judgment: the Judge will not ask us about how we handled the Bible, but only whether we responded affirmatively to his word that came to us in the need of the "least of his brethren."

6. Conclusion

With a variation on a familiar Dutch proverb, one can say: Every believer has his text (Translator's note: the Dutch proverb is "Elke ketter heeft zijn letter"; literally, "every heretic has his letter," i. e., everyone knows how to cite a biblical text to support his own divergent view.). We have seen in a great many examples how in earlier times people twisted biblical texts to suit themselves. The historical approach involves our seeking for what was meant by those who stand behind the texts. We found that the essential element in Israel's experience with God came to expression in Jesus in such a way that he could become the center of a universal human community.

Of course it is the ideas and ideals of our own time that open our eyes to this reality, and it is the needs and distresses of our world which cause us to believe in this Jesus as the only one who can give us a future. This faith in Jesus, in whom the fellowship-founding character of God takes shape for us, brings us together in the framework of a new confessionalism. Only in this perspective can biblical texts function with authority.

It is evident that the Bible most fully receives its due in the observance of the Lord's Supper, or the Eucharist, wherein we accept Jesus' invitation to find each other in table-fellowship with him and in so doing to make a highly significant beginning toward what must become the whole of humanity.

As texts to read in that setting, our attention is drawn first of all to those in which his intentions, commands, and promises are most expressively stated. It was precisely this proclamation that brought him into the situation which we commemorate, "the night before he was to suffer...."

Narrative passages from the gospels and passages from the

other writings of the New Testament can accompany this reading, so long as they are unmistakably placed in the service of Jesus' intentions for those present. This must be much more strongly emphasized with reference to passages from the Old Testament. Of course everything depends here on the degree to which those present are familiar with the biblical texts and themes and the biblical ways of conceiving things and what they can provide that is of interest for the exposition of these texts.

A basic principle should be that mystification is avoided, and that a text is used only when something of its real intention can show through. It is *not* required that everything always must be completely clear. Ultimately here we have to do with the mysteries of existence, and the language that is used here can only be that of faith and love.

It is this fact above all that restrains me from giving more concrete directions and suggestions. We shall have to come jointly to a use of the Bible which no longer divides, but unites us. This must be the case also in the sense that it is not limited to a group of initiates who are able to digest all sorts of "difficulties," but is accessible to everyone who is motivated by what inspired Jesus.

Notes

Page 1   The story about the Koran is found in G. van der Leeuw, *Phänomenologie der Religion*, Tübingen, second edition, 1956, p. 500, n. 1.

Page 7   J. Bright, *A History of Israel*, Philadelphia, 1959, p. 416. The term *dies natalis* comes from A. Gelin, in the volume entitled *Moise, l'homme de l'Alliance*, Paris, 1955, p. 51.

Pages 8, 9   The quotations are from Ecclesiasticus (or Sirach) 24:7-23 and Baruch 3:31-4:1. Both books are found in Catholic editions of the Bible, but not in most Protestant editions. Cf. further the note related to p. 120.

Page 10   I have drawn these rabbinical texts about the Torah from E. Schürer, *Geschichte des jüdischen Volkes*, Leipzig, fourth edition, 1907, pp. 365 f., and from W. Bousset, *Die Religion des Judentums im späthellenistischen Zeitalter*, Tübingen, third edition, 1926, p. 121.

Page 10   The "Book of Jubilees" is found in R. H. Charles, *The Apocrypha and Pseudepigrapha of the Old Testament*, London, 1913, Vol. II, pp. 1-82.

Page 13   The text from Exodus 21:22-23 is discussed by Th. Beemer in a study of "Abortus provocatus en de waarde van het menselijk leven," in *Tijdschrift voor Theologie* 10 (1970), pp. 280 f.

Page 14   For the letter of Aristeas I have used the edition by A. Pelletier, *Lettre d'Aristée à Philocrate*, Paris, 1962. The introduction treats, among other matters, the development of the legend, beginning with Philo, p. 78 f. [Note: the work is available in English in an edition by Moses Hadas, *Aristeas to Philocrates (Letter of Aristeas)*, 1951. Tr.]

Page 18   F. Weinreb, *De Bijbel als schepping*, Den Haag, 1963, pp. 331 and 45.

Pages 19, 20   Aristeas, sections 142 ff.

Page 21   The quotation is found in Philo's writing "On Cain's posterity." It is also found in the long quotation given by C. K. Barrett in

175

The New Testament Background: Selected Documents, New York, 1957, pp. 180-82.

Page 22   I found Philo's interpretation of the three patriarchs described by J. Daniélou, *Philon d'Alexandrie*, Paris, 1957, pp. 138 ff.

Page 22   C. Siegfried's twenty-three rules are listed by F. Schröger, *Der Verfasser des Hebräerbriefes als Schriftausleger*, Regensburg, 1968, pp. 293-301.

Page 25   This book attributed to Ezra is found in R. H. Charles, in the work cited above, as IV Ezra (Vol. II, pp. 542-624).

Pages 27, 28   The translation of the commentaries on Habakkuk and Psalm 37 follows that of Dr. A. S. van der Woude, *Bijbelcommentaren en bijbelse verhalen*, Amsterdam, 1958, a part of the series *De handschriften van de Dode Zee in Nederlandse Vertaling*.

Page 28   The quotation is from the English translation of Joseph Klausner's *Jesus of Nazareth* (originally written in Hebrew), London, 1925, p. 376. My attention was called to it years ago in a book by C. H. Dodd, who has recently used it again in his *The Founder of Christianity*, London, 1970, pp. 77 f.

Page 29   The quotation is from I Maccabees 4:46. See also 14:41.

Page 33   The saying about the sick and the physician is in Luke 5:31, and the call of Zacchaeus in Luke 19:8.

Page 34   The story of the Samaritan is in Luke 10:25-37.

Page 37   About unlimited forgiveness, Matthew 18:21-35.

Page 40   The sabbath is made for man, Mark 2:27. What makes a man unclean, Mark 7:15.

Page 41   The story of the woman taken in adultery has been preserved in some manuscripts of the Fourth Gospel, John 8:1-11.

Page 43   Jesus' saying about preeminence and service in Luke 22:24-27.

Page 46   Peter recognizes in Jesus the Messiah, Mark 8:29. A trace of this ecstatic captivation is preserved in John 6:15. Jesus made Lord and Messiah, Acts 2:36.

Page 47   Egyptian illustrations of Psalm 110 in my *Shorter Atlas of the Bible*, Edinburgh, 1959, p. 90; commentary on p. 91.

Pages 48, 49   The promises of Nathan in II Samuel 7:14. Israel as God's son and firstborn, Exodus 4:22-23. Further in Hosea 11:1; Isaiah 1:2; Jeremiah 3:19, and the great prayer in Isaiah 63:15-64:12. Texts from the Book of Wisdom 2:13-20.

Pages 49, 50   The words of Jesus from Matthew 7:9-11; Luke 12:49-50; Mark 9:19; and again Matthew 11:27.

Pages 51, 52   Proverbs 8:22 f. Paul on the love of God in Romans 8:31-32, and John in his first epistle, 4:7-9.

Page 53   The prophecies in Micah 5:1-3 and Isaiah 7:14.

Page 54   Joel 2:28-32 (in some Bibles 3:1-5) is quoted in Acts 2:17-21.

Pages 58, 59   The story of the manna in Exodus 16 and Number 11. Elisha in II Kings 5:42-44. Jesus in Mark 6:30-44 and 8:1-8. The stilling of the storm in Mark 4:35-41 and the transfiguration in Luke 9:28-36.

Page 61   Darkness at noon in Amos 8:9-10.

Page 62, 63   The curse upon one who hangs on a tree in Deuteronomy 21:23, cited by Paul in Galatians 3:13. The allusion to Isaiah 49 in Galatians 2:15.

Page 64   About Abraham's faith, Romans 4:9-12 and 17-22.

Pages 64, 65   Fellow-heirs with Christ, Romans 8:17. The text from Genesis 12:7 is employed in Galatians 3:16.

Pages 65, 66   About the two sons of Abraham, Galatians 4:21-31. The threshing ox in Deuteronomy 25:4, mentioned in I Corinthians 9:9.

Page 67   James 2:20-26.

Page 68   Paul, speaking about the veil worn by Moses, in II Corinthians 3:4-17.

Page 69   Paul on our knowledge of God, in I Corinthians 13:8-12.

Pages 71, 72   The quotation is from Beryl Smalley, *The Study of the Bible in the Middle Ages*, Oxford, 1952, p. 14. Origen's sermon here follows the edition in *Sources Chrétienne, Origène, Homélies sur l'Exode*, Paris, 1947, pp. 98 f. The "prophet" quoted by Origen is Psalm 45:11.

Page 73   I have drawn Origen's reflections on the transfiguration from H. de Lubac, *Historie et Esprit*, Paris, 1950, p. 276, and from an article by J. Guillet in *Recherches de Science Religieuse* 34 (1947), p. 292.

Page 74   From the sermon on Exodus cited above, p. 334. Origen quotes John 15:16 and Matthew 12:29.

Pages 74-76   The sermons on Joshua are from *Origènes, Homélies sur Josue*, Paris, 1960, pp. 101, 118 f., and 341 f. Origen is quoting either Proverbs 26:11 or II Peter 2:22. See also Luke 11:26. The reference to the little children of Babylon is taken from the close of Psalm 137, and that to evil thoughts from Matthew 15:19. According to Genesis 11:9, Babel means "confusion."

Page 78   From Origen's sermon on Joshua, in the work cited above, pp. 137 f.

Page 79   Rahab in Matthew 1:5, Hebrews 11:31, and James 2:25.

Pages 79, 80   The texts from Clement, Justin, and Irenaeus according to J. Danielou, *Sacramentum Futuri*, Paris, 1950, pp. 217 f.

Page 82   Quotations are from the book by H. Lubac, pp. 207 f.

Pages 82, 83   Gregory's exposition according to H. Tissot, *Les Pères vous parlent de l'Evangile*, Paris, 1953, pp. 686 f.

Page 83   The interpretation of the Good Samaritan follows that of L. Billot, *De Ecclesiae Sacramentis*, Rom, 1931, pp. 7-9.

Page 85   From J. Huizinga, *The Waning of the Middle Ages*, 1924, p. 187.

Pages 86, 87   Following the sample translation of this *enarratio* in *Tijdschrift voor geestelijk leven*, 14 (1958), pp. 665-76.

Page 88   Thomas is quoted following the "Opera Omnia" edition of Vivès, Part 18, p. 228.

Pages 89, 90   I have quoted Erasmus from a study by E. Kohls, *Die Theologie des Erasmus*, Basel, 1966, pp. 126 f.

Page 91   Yves Congar, "The Sacralization of Western Society in the

Middle Ages," in *Sacralization and Secularization* (*Concilium*, Vol. 47, 1969), pp. 55-71.

Page 92   Yves Congar, "Ecce constitui te super gentes et regna etc.," in the Festschrift edited by Michael Schmaus, *Theologie in Geschichte und Gegenwart*, Munchen, 1957, pp. 671-96. The letter of Charlemagne follows J. Lecler, "L'argument des deux glaives," in *Recherches de Science Religieuse*, 21 (1931), pp. 299-339.

Page 93   The information about the use of the Bible in connection with the Crusades is found in P. Rousset, *Les origines et les caractères de la première croisade*, Neuchâtel, 1945.

Page 94   The quotations are from L. Hanke, *The Spanish Struggle for Justice in the Conquest of America*, Philadelphia, 1949, pp. 31 f. and 120 f.

Page 96   I read the book *Het leesgezelschap van Diepenbeek* in the edition of the *Bibliotheek der Nederlandse Letteren*, Amsterdam, 1939.

Page 97   My attention was called to the role of Niebuhr by S. Neill, *The Interpretation of the New Testament*, London, 1964, p. 7.

Page 99   I found the statement by Lutz in an article by A. Bea, in *Biblica*, 40 (1959), p. 325. Wellhausen's letter is in H.-J. Kraus, *Geschichte der historisch-kritischen Erforschung des Alten Testaments*, Neukirchen, 1956, p. 236.

Pages 99, 100   The statement that Moses himself wrote is found, among other places, in Exodus 17:14; 24:4; 34:27 f.; Numbers 33:2; and Deuteronomy 31:19, 22. The transfiguration of Christ in John 5:45-47.

Pages 103, 104   The information about Poels is taken from his biography by J. Colsen, *Poels*, Roermond, 1955, pp. 85-110. Later on in the same book the author describes how Poels' professorship at the Catholic University in Washington was made impossible by agitation from the side of orthodoxy. Is it accidental that this devoted biblical scholar became the great champion of the social movement in Limburg?

Pages 104, 105   Any Catholic theologian will have the *Responsiones* of the Papal Biblical Commission in his copy of Denzinger, *Enchiridion Symbolorum*, published in a new revision every few years at Freiburg im Breisgau. This book also contains the *Motu proprio* of November 18, 1907, and the most important passages of the encyclicals cited.

Page 107   Aalders' *Oudtestamentische Kanoniek* was published in Kampen by J. H. Kok Uitgeversmaatschappij N.V.

Page 112   The quotation is from J. S. van der Ploeg, *Les Chants du Serviteur de Jahve*, Paris, 1936, p. 16.

Pages 112, 113   From Aalders' work, pp. 214, 215, and 218; the italics are mine.

Page 116   The reference here is to J. Goettsberger, *Die Bucher der Chronik oder Paralipomenon*, Bonn, 1939; the quotations are from pp. 16, 17, and 159. That the new approach to Chronicles can help in the explanation of the nature of the gospels I have shown in *Tijdschrift voor Theologie*, 4 (1964), pp. 35-53, "De historiciteit der evangeliën toegelicht door het Oude Testament."

Pages 117, 118   *The Jerusalem Bible*, Garden City, N.Y., 1966, pp. 492-93.

Page 120   The apocryphal books are now available in *The Oxford Annotated Apocrypha*, New York, 1965, and *The New Oxford Annotated Bible with the Apocrypha*, New York, 1973.

Page 122   The story about the preaching comes from *Theologische Zeitschrift*, 12 (1956), p. 431. I have also used it in a detailed description of the contemporary debates over the significance of the Old Testament in *Tijdschrift voor Theologie*, 2 (1962), pp. 316-50.

Page 125   L. Fonck, *Der Kampf um die Wahrheit der Heiligen Schrift seit 25 Jahren*, Innsbruck, 1905, p. 202.

Pages 126, 127   The series of articles by Werner Harenberg in *Der Spiegel* appeared later in book form. The title in English is *Der Spiegel on the New Testament* (1970), and the quotations are from pp. 4 and 192.

Page 130   *The Bible in Modern Scholarship*, P. Hyatt, editor, Nashville, 1965, p. 11.

Page 132   The Scandinavian scholar referred to here is K. Stendahl, in "The Apostle Paul and the Introspective Conscience of the West," a contribution to *Ecumenical Dialogue at Harvard*, Cambridge, 1964.

Page 133   B. van Iersel, "De heilshistorische betekenis van Israel," in *Kosmos en Oecumene*, 4 (1970), p. 315.

Page 135   The texts from Thomas Aquinas are in G. Kreling, *Het goddelijk geheim in de theologie*, Nijmegen, 1939.

Page 136   R. Guardini, *Aards en hemels heil*, Utrecht, 1949, pp. 14 f.

Page 138   This is a summary following P. Ellis, *The Yahwist*, Notre Dame, 1968.

Page 143   Hosea 4:2; Amos 9:7 and 3:12.

Page 145   J. Renckens, *De profeet van de Nabijheid Gods*, Tielt, 1961, pp. 158 f.

Page 147   Jeremiah 7:9.

Page 149   Deuteronomy 20:18.

Pages 151, 152   J. Renckens, *De godsdienst van Israel*, Roermond, 1962, pp. 243 f.

Page 153   W. D. Davies, *Paul and Rabbinic Judaism*, London, 1965, pp. 63 f.

Page 155   E. R. Dodds, *Pagan and Christian in an Age of Anxiety*, Cambridge, 1965, pp. 137 f. The reference to Festugière is also found there.

Page 156   A. D. Nock, *Conversion*, Oxford, 1969, p. 210.

Page 158   F. Tellegen, in *Katholiek Artsenblad*, 1969, pp. 180 f.

Page 166   H. Berkhof, in the volume entitled *Geloven in God*, Den Haag, 1970, p. 124.

Page 169   J. Petuchowsky, *Zion Reconsidered*, New York, 1966, p. 8.